When Rover Just Won't Do

When Rover Just Won't Do

Over 2,000 Suggestions for Naming Your Puppy

Danny Scalisi

AND

Libby Moses

HOWELL
BOOK HOUSE

New York

Maxwell Macmillan Canada
Toronto

Maxwell Macmillan International
New York   Oxford   Singapore   Sydney

Howell Book House
Macmillan Publishing Company
866 Third Avenue
New York, NY 10022

Maxwell Macmillan Canada, Inc.
1200 Eglinton Avenue East
Suite 200
Don Mills, Ontario M3C 3N1

Macmillan Publishing Company is part of the Maxwell Communication Group of Companies.

Library of Congress Cataloging-in-Publication Data

Scalisi, Danny.
When Rover just won't do : over 2,000 suggestions for naming your puppy / Danny Scalisi and Libby Moses.
p. cm.
ISBN 0-87605-691-5
1. Dogs—Names. I. Moses, Libby. II. Title.
SF422.3.S33   1993   92-43503
636.7'0887—dc20   CIP

Macmillan books are available at special discounts for bulk purchases for sales promotions, premiums, fund-raising, or educational use. For details, contact:

Special Sales Director
Macmillan Publishing Company
866 Third Avenue
New York, NY 10022

10 9 8 7 6 5 4 3 2 1

Printed in the United States of America

*Dedicated to Matilda the Doberman Pinscher,
whose stubbornness taught us more
about dog behavior than we ever wanted
to know, and to Delilah the Bulldog, whose babies
were the inspiration for all our work.*

Contents

Acknowledgments

SPECIAL THANKS to Theodore Hayes, D.V.M., whose knowledge, expertise, insight and exceptional humor could inspire anyone to love animals. Without Dr. Hayes, Maxine Ray, D.V.M., Veterinary Technician Jenny Klenke and all the staff of Southtown Veterinary Hospital, this book would not have been possible.

John F. and Susan B. McGibbon, owners of J.B. Rare Bulldogs, as well as breeders and handlers, are truly our special mentors in Bulldogs. Without them the world would not only be lacking this book, but also some of the most beautiful Bulldogs that ever happened.

Another veterinarian who has made significant contributions to both the construction of this book and to the constant struggle for sound, healthy animals is Alfred Plechner, D.V.M., and his staff at California Animal Hospital.

All the crazy dog people at the Laurel Canyon Dog Park contributed not only by diligently providing a host of terrific names, but most important, by being the canine fanatics that they truly are. The world would not be as nice a place without them and this wonderful park.

Wade Stinson and his Rottweiler Morgan also deserve mention.

Jeff and Radar Doroshkin were saviors in our time of computer desperation.

The many creative names and messages left on our machine by Luca Scalisi will not go unforgotten. We may have converted him into a dog person after all.

Chris Moses, pig and snake lover, computer-literate person and brother, helped greatly in the research aspects of this book. Without his computer expertise there would have been no hope of completing the project. He might even have influenced a tad of the humor. *See* BACON *in Chapter 2.*

It is also necessary for me, Libby Moses, to thank my mother and father, not only because if I fail to do so I will never hear the end of it, but because without them I would never have learned the beauty of wallowing in puppy pens, sleeping with guinea pigs, swimming with dolphins and having a reptilian brother.

Introduction
....

PARENTS-TO-BE often contemplate names, and sometimes careers, for their babies long before the new family member is even born. Their child will be wearing this name for a lifetime so they have an important responsibility. This responsibility is by no means easier for new dog owners. Whether your new family member is a puppy or adult dog, you can expect the dog to carry its name for a lifetime.

This book is designed to help you name your dog. It lists thousands of names—with brief definitions, anecdotal depictions of their origin, or attributes associated with them. Also included are names of famous and successful people and fictional characters with which to dub your pet, as well as names that suit particular breeds of dogs. In addition, dog owners with two or more dogs will find popular and novel names to suit their situation. In the final portion of this introduction you will find pointers on familiarizing your pooch with his or her new name.

WHAT'S IN A NAME?

It is evident that people have strong and direct impressions about what sort of pooch will have a certain name. For instance, "Cuddles" brings to mind a furry lap dog, who

wiggles ecstatically at first sight of her owner as she charades for affection. Hence, the name itself makes your pet
all the more lovable. But a common, uninspired name can
signify a pet taken for granted, one relegated to the confines
of the yard and hardly regarded as a special family member
at all. Names, therefore, have a significant impact on how
others will react to your pet. Hearing an endearing, individual
name, or learning that a dog was named after an appealing
fictional character or an accomplished relative might boost
someone's opinion of the animal and in turn provide the
pet with greater appreciation and love, which is, of course,
the ultimate goal.

In the immediate moment of consuming joy, when
your puppy arrives home for the first time, as you cuddle
the puppy and coo into his or her fuzzy ears, you should not
be hasty with picking a name. An immediate, miscalculated,
creative impulse, seemingly logical at first, can wear thin
with time. Choosing the name should be done before your
four-legged friend arrives in your home or after you have
adequately observed some of his or her physical characteristics and personality traits.

If your decision is an inspiration based on the animal's
physical characteristics (i.e., Brownie or Spot) make sure
these are traits that will not change. For example, "Wrinkles"
the Chinese Shar-Pei may be a cute ball of loose skin at
eight weeks, but at eight years she will look more like a wolf
than a bundle of ripples and the name will simply make no
sense. This can also be the case with dogs named after
popular media personalities. Although personalities might
fade (i.e., "Ollie" as in Oliver North), don't let the affection
for your dog fade with the fad. Puppies are not passing
trends.

GETTING OFF ON THE RIGHT PAW

Teaching your new dog his or her name is as important as
choosing it. It is tempting, especially with a puppy, to shorten

the name into a nickname, most commonly by dropping the last letter or syllable of the original name and adding to it "y," "ie" or "ette." "Sunshine" quickly becomes "Sunny," and "Rosebud," "Rosey." For training purposes it is best to avoid this. Familiarizing your dog with his or her name is essential. If "Scooter" becomes "Scooty-wootey" every time except when you are angry at him or trying to enforce a command, he will become confused and never learn to obey you. Try to use his *real* name even when speaking affectionately. Furthermore, you will find your dog more obedient if you use his *real* name to get his attention before a command.

Most importantly, simply use the name and use it often! Say it with different intonations in your voice so the dog becomes accustomed to the word and not just your tone. Introduce your dog as you would a family member to visitors. Have the visitors use the name, so the pet gets used to various voices and learns to be responsive in widely varying circumstances. This technique could help save your dog's life. In the event your puppy is lost or in danger, he or she may have to one day rely on and listen for his or her name being called as a vehicle to safety—perhaps by a stranger.

Your dog's name is limited only by your imagination.

1

A Pup with Meaning

ALEXANDER POPE WROTE, "Histories are more full of examples of the fidelity of dogs than of friends." In this chapter the history and meaning of many names are given for pet owners who want something more behind a faithful pup than just a cute, cuddly sweet nothing. These are names with meanings, and whether the meaning is a foreign translation or definition, it is seasoned with whimsical suggestions for how the canine bearing this name might look or act.

ADRIATIC This offshoot of the Mediterranean Sea is known for its connection to the main port of Venice, Italy. It could be a good name for an Italian Greyhound or Maltese.

AKIRA "Brightness" in Japanese. Pronounced *A-Kee-Da* in English, hence, a logical name for an Akita.

ALCATRAZ No bars will be able to confine this crafty pup, not even the old maximum security federal penitentiary just offshore in the San Francisco Bay.

ALCHEMY The goal of this antiquated chemical philosophy was to change base metals into gold. This is a good name for a puppy brought home from the pound. His life was transformed from one of leaden prospects to one with a golden future. His gratitude and love will undoubtedly enrich your life.

ALEXIA The loss of ability to read. Be patient; this puppy might be a slow learner, but she'll come through as gracefully as her name indicates.

ALLEGRO "Cheerful" in Italian and "happy" in Spanish (spelled ALEGRE), both of which may epitomize your dog. If you look hard you might just catch him smile.

ALPACA An animal from South America, related to the llama, which has a slender neck and thick, woolly coat. This is an intriguing name for a Poodle or any dog with these physical traits.

ALPHA This is the first letter of the Greek alphabet and a word that denotes the first of anything. Does he or she have first and final say in your household?

AMABLE Meaning "kind" in Spanish. Most any puppy, especially a sleeping one, will fit this description.

AMAZON In Greek mythology this was a race of fighting women who are thought to have dwelled close to the Black Sea. They were supposedly large, strong and unyielding. If your dog fits, use it.

AMBER A brownish yellow color. Good name for a Golden Retriever or any dog of similar coloring.

AMBROSIA In Greek and Roman mythology this was the food of the gods and, aside from being fragrant, it supposedly created immortality. This puppy's love will be equally as satisfying and everlasting.

AMIGO "Friend" in Spanish. Your puppy makes it easy to see why dogs are deservedly considered man's best friend.

AMMO Short for "ammunition." Well-trained guard and protection dogs are perfect examples and candidates. It might also be a good name for a future hunting companion.

AMORE "Love" in Italian. If you give a little, you will get a lot from any puppy in any language.

ANACONDA A nonvenomous snake that resembles a very large boa constrictor and which crushes and strangles its prey. This is a good name for a pup whose notion of cuddling might be a bit constricting.

ANDALUSIA A mountainous region of southern Spain. Enchanting and warm are qualities of both this area and your puppy so named.

ANDORRA This small country lies in the East Pyrenees between France and Spain. Good name for a Great Pyrenees.

ANDROID An artificial person with extremely humanlike features. There is a good chance that a pup with this name thinks human food and bed are not out of line.

ANGSTROM A hundred-millionth of a centimeter. Good name for a Chihuahua, or any very small dog.

APACHE A formerly nomadic tribe of North American Indians. For a puppy who will disappear on long wandering crusades if you forget to close the gate.

APOGEE The farthest point. A puppy with this name will go to all extremes to please you.

APRIL The fourth month of the Gregorian calendar. Good name for a puppy born during this month or one who might just bring some flowering beauty to your life all year long.

AQUARIUS In Latin, this eleventh sign of the zodiac means literally "water carrier." Good name for any dog that loves a splashing good time, whether it be in the pool, ocean or bathtub.

ARAPAHO A tribe of North American Indians now living in the Pacific Northwest. This is a good name for a rugged, outdoor dog.

ARIES The first sign of the zodiac. It translates to "ram." This is a good name for a male puppy born under this sign or having a bold, "ramlike" personality.

ASPEN A tree whose leaves shake or quiver in the wind. Whippets can appear equally as lithe and delicate.

ATLANTIS This legendary island is thought to have sunken in the Atlantic. A natural-born swimmer such as a Labrador, Newfoundland or Golden Retriever could be properly adorned with this name.

AUGUST The eighth month of the year. Named after Augustus Caesar. An appropriate name for a puppy born this month.

AUREOLE An illuminated glow around a body, which at times signifies holiness. Is there a halo around the head of your slipper-chewing, carpet-staining devil?

AVALON A paradise thought to exist during the time of King Arthur. A pup with this name might be reminiscent of such idyllic beauty.

AVANTI Italian for "forward." This name is appropriate for an overtly flirtatious puppy.

AXLE Divine reward or source of life. You must have done something good to deserve such a special puppy. Possibly you adopted him from the local shelter.

BABIRUSA A wild pig from Ceylon, much like your trash-rooting, mud-slinging puppy.

BABUSHKA "Grandmother" in Russian. A puppy with this name will always do her best to take care of you.

BACCARAT A card game; however, this pup might not be holding a full deck.

BACI "Kisses" in Italian. All puppies love to give them.

BAGUETTE A French roll. A puppy of any nationality would love to share yours.

BAILEY The encasing of a castle. A puppy with this name will be protective and loyal.

BAJA "Short" or "low" in Spanish, humorously suits your Great Dane puppy and seriously suits your Basset Hound.

BALDRIC Old English for "valiant" and "courageous." Good name for an Old English Sheepdog or any self-assured pup.

BALI This South Indonesian island and its residents are known for their lovely music and dancing. An equally beautiful and festive puppy is deserving of this name.

BAMBINO "Child" or "baby" in Italian. Any small puppy could be named this, however it is particularly appropriate for dogs that remain small and puppylike all their lives, such as Yorkshire Terriers.

BANDITO "Bandit" or "brigand" in Spanish. Usually traveling in packs, they are a looting group of outlaws. Good for the pup whose idea of fun is pillaging your home.

BANGLE A decorative bracelet or anklet. A puppy profoundly attached to you might be appropriate for this name.

BANZAI Originally known as a Japanese scream of patriotism or a possible forewarning to imminent destruction. This pup's cries should be taken seriously.

BARNACLE A marine crustacean or, simply put, a bump on a log. This puppy might need some motivating.

BARON The lowest echelon of nobility and a good name for a puppy that can be a royal pain!

BAROQUE An art and architecture style developed in Europe during the sixteenth century. It is represented by elaborate, ornate, rich and powerful styles. Good for any dog that fits the description.

BASEL A city in Switzerland. Good name for a Bernese Mountain Dog or a Saint Bernard.

BASIL An herb having fragrant leaves and commonly used as a kitchen spice. Your puppy is the spice of your life.

BEAU The steady companion of a girl. Disarmingly charming, this pup will melt most female hearts.

BEAUCOUP "Much" in French. Typifies a very expensive pup, who was, of course, worth every penny!

BEDOUIN A member of a nomadic Arab tribe that is known to be heat-tolerant and have extremely well-developed survival instincts. Good name for a Saluki.

BEEFEATER Originally a guard of English monarchy, this puppy inherently knows how to protect you.

BEELZEBUB Latin for "devil." *See* DEVIL *in Chapter 2.*

BELLA MIA Italian feminine for "my beautiful one." It is hard to be objective with this pup.

BELLADONNA A poisonous European plant. There is no serum to protect you from extreme attachment to this pup. You really wouldn't want one anyway.

BELLE French for "beautiful." Beauty is in the eye of the beholder; therefore this is a humorous name for dogs that are considered beautiful only on the inside and an admiring name for dogs that are beautiful to all.

BELUGA The eggs of the sturgeon native to the Black Sea or Caspian Sea make some of the world's best and most expensive caviar. Good name for a Borzoi.

BENGAL Inspired by the Bengal tiger, the largest cat of India. A courageous, awe-inspiring puppy with an aura of supreme self-assurance deserves this name.

BEOWOOF This name is derived from the Old English epic *Beowulf*, dating from about the year 700, perhaps the most important surviving work of the Anglo-Saxon period. In this historical poem the hero, Beowulf, slays two dreaded dragons, but in doing so is killed himself. A doggie with this name has some pretty big paws to fill.

BERET A popular French cap. Good name for a Papillon or French Bulldog.

BETA Second letter of the Greek alphabet or the second in any type of list. Good name for the second dog of the household.

BEULAH A land of peace. Since your pup's arrival, you have yearned for a tranquil existence.

BIALY A baked roll, much like a bagel, covered with onion flakes. This puppy can't wait to be buttered up with toys and love.

BIANCO or BIANCA Italian for "white." Perfect for a Bichon Frise, Maltese, Samoyed or West Highland White Terrier.

BIG DIPPER A cluster of seven stars known for its brightness and unique formation. Your puppy can probably measure up to this constellation with his or her bright, shiny eyes and stellar personality.

BIJOU French for "jewel." Appropriate for any small dog with a dazzling personality.

BOA A large snake known to coil and suffocate its prey. The only thing this pup might suffocate you with is affection.

BOBO A dolt or dunce. Although a slow learner, this puppy will come around. Besides, brains aren't everything.

BOCA Spanish for "mouth." Good for pups with inherently big ones.

BODHI or BODHISATTVA Enlightenment; one who forgoes enlightenment in order to save others. A selfless, fearless puppy.

BOHEMIAN An artistic or literary character who refuses to conform to conventional standards of behavior and instead chooses to drink from the toilet and lick plates clean.

BOLL WEEVIL A strange-looking, long-nosed beetle, but she's still beautiful to you.

BONSAI Dwarfed, decoratively shaped trees or shrubs grown in miniature pots. Good for naturally dwarfed pups such as the Chihuahua or Yorkshire Terrier.

BORA This tumultuous cold wind blows on the Dalmatian coast of Yugoslavia in winter. This might resemble the freezing drafts caused by your Dalmatian puppy blowing in and out of his or her doggie door.

BORSCHT Beet soup. A taste for this pup might be something you have to acquire.

BOUBIE or **BOUBA** A Yiddish word for "grandmother." *See* BABUSHKA.

BOUFFANT To be puffed out in a full fashion. Definitely fits a well-groomed Poodle, as well as some other breeds.

BOUGAINVILLEA A plant with small, colorfully arranged flowers, named after Louis Antoine de Bougainville. Whatever the setting, this pup makes a striking impression.

BOXER A person who fights with the fists. This pushy pup can get you into a lot of trouble at the park.

BRIE A type of soft cheese named after a region of France. Nice name for a puppy with epicurean leanings.

BRIER A thorny-stemmed plant. Good for the wire-haired breeds.

BRITTANY This peninsula is between the English Channel and the Bay of Biscay; however, this name also applies to an area of northwest France. Good name for a Brittany or any other dog.

BUCKEYE An oversized nut from the chestnut family. Instead of tennis balls or Frisbees this puppy probably earned his name by chasing buckeyes.

BUCKHEAD A Georgia city, or just a cute name for a puppy who seems slightly dense at times.

BUCKINGHAM The royal palace in London, England, is well protected, just like your home since this loyal, protective guard puppy arrived.

BUCKO Meaning "a bully." Tongue-in-cheek name for a timid, sheepish puppy. It might just help build up his confidence.

BURGUNDY Red or white wines made in the Burgundy region of France, also the deep red color. Like a fine wine, your puppy will improve with age.

BURMA This Southeast Asian republic lies east of the Bay of Bengal. A puppy with this name brings to mind the allure of exotic places and he or she will gladly travel with you.

BUZZARD This name can describe a bird of prey or a person or puppy with a large appetite.

BYTE A small, powerful unit of computer memory. Reprogramming may be in order if he or she doesn't learn obedience commands.

C.E.O. This canine chief executive officer is destined to run your life.

C'EST MOI French for "It's me." An extroverted puppy who likes to be the center of attention.

CABO Short for Cabo San Lucas, a Mexican city at the tip of the Baja Peninsula, which could well be where a stranded puppy could come from.

CADBURY The trademark name for an English sweets company known for its deliciously rich chocolate. Good name for a chocolate Labrador, red Doberman Pinscher or any deep brown, smooth-coated puppy.

CADDY A golfer's attendant. This particular pup is always ready to help and could play fetch all day long.

CADENCE Having a recurring, regular beat or flow. Watching this puppy move and bark is sheer poetry in motion.

CALICO This word describes a dappled or speckled color scheme. A piebald puppy would be perfect for this name.

CAMELOT This is the legendary site where King Arthur had his Round Table. Many heroes have come from this place. Maybe your pup will measure up to their greatness.

CANIS "Dog" in Latin. *See* Dog.

CAPO Italian for "boss" or "head." This puppy has a harder time taking orders than most.

CAPRICORN This tenth sign of the zodiac depicts a horned goat. Good name for a puppy who climbs on furniture as if it were mountains and who eats most anything.

CAPTAIN A leader of a military body, or maybe just your household.

CARIBOU This member of the deer family is indigenous to Northern Canada, Alaska and Arctic regions of the Western Hemisphere. This big-eared puppy probably likes to play in the snow just like his namesake.

CASBAH A stronghold or castle normally associated with Northern Africa. Good name for a large, rather protective guard dog of any breed.

CASHMERE A breed of goat, found mainly in India, that produces a type of soft wool regarded among the finest quality available. Good for dogs with soft cashmere-like hair.

CASINO Meaning "gambling establishment" in English and "confusion" in Italian; however, your pup doesn't have to be Italian to earn this name. The housebreaking stage defies international borders and is always a venture that can have you guessing until the wheel stops.

CASPIAN Meaning "lionlike appearance." This is a good name for a Little Lion Dog.

CASSIS The dark berries of this plant are used to make a flavorful after-dinner drink of the same name. Your pup's deep, rich-colored coat might make this name appropriate.

CATALINA A small island some twenty-five miles west of Long Beach, California, known for its romantic tourist appeal. A pup bearing this name will anxiously await your weekends away together.

CAVIAR Fish eggs served primarily as an appetizer or hors d'oeuvre. This delicacy, like your puppy, may take some time to get used to.

CHA SU BAO A Chinese barbecued, pork-filled dumpling. *See* DUMPLING *in Chapter 2.*

CHAMBRAY A delicate type of fabric made with white fibers. A puppy with this name must have an extremely soft coat.

CHAMOIS Soft leather derived from the yellowish tan skin of the European mountain goat of the same name. Great for any pups of similar coloring and with "stroke-able" coats. The yellow Labrador, Golden Retriever and Soft Coated Wheaten Terrier are logical candidates.

CHAYA From the Hebrew meaning "to be alive." A puppy's zest for life never ceases, except during nap time and even then he's twitching!

CHECCA A traditional Italian appetizer usually prepared with lots of garlic. You can take this pup in small doses only.

CHEETAH This slender cat is known for its ability to achieve tremendous speed. A pup with this potential might give the idea of taking a walk a whole new meaning.

CHERUB A winged, angelic entity. Your puppy may not fit this name now, but it has been said that babies grow into their names so maybe it's worth a try.

CHEYENNE Fighter, powerful, strong, needs to run. The Sioux Indians originally named this tribe "Shi-hen-na" for the red paint used on their faces. Great for an Irish Setter or red Doberman Pinscher.

CHIANTI Red wine from the Italian mountains, also a tasteful name for a Papillon, Italian Greyhound or even a Neapolitan Mastiff.

CHICO "Small" in Spanish. Great tongue-in-cheek name for any dog of the giant breeds.

CHIFFON A sheer, ornamental fabric that has a light, delicate consistency, like the smaller Toy breeds who can highlight an outfit by peeking out of a handbag or delicately posing in Mommy's arms.

CHINCHILLA This small, gray South American rodent is a relative of the squirrel. Good name for a lush-coated Toy dog.

CHIQUITA The feminine derivative of "small" in Spanish. This name is equally good for large or small dogs, or those with an affinity for bananas.

CHIVAS Old, rare scotch that is probably too expensive for you to share with even your best friend, your Scottish Terrier.

CHOCTAW A tribe of Indians originally located in Alabama, Louisiana and Mississippi. Good name for a Southern dog such as the Redbone Coonhound.

CHOLO Spanish slang for "local menace." This pup will probably not have a problem living up to his name.

CHOPPER Slang for "helicopter." Landings can be dangerous for puppies who clumsily leap on and off the furniture.

CHORIZO A highly seasoned pork sausage. Legs that look like pork chops and a sausage-shaped body? Sound familiar to any of you owners of little guys?

CHOTCHKE A Yiddish word for bric-a-brac; also a term of endearment for a child, sweetheart or puppy, sometimes delivered tongue-in-cheek.

CHOW MEIN A Chinese-American combination food dish. Your fortune says you should get a Chinese Shar-Pei, Chow Chow, Pekingese or Pug.

CHUTNEY A jamlike spice made with fruits and onions. It is typically served with Indian food, but your puppy wouldn't mind it on his dinner.

CHUTZPA Yiddish for "brashness." Puppies' strong wills are hard to change and this name is appropriate for any brazen pup who likes to do things his or her own way.

CIAO A way to say "good-bye" or "hello" in Italian. Good for a Chow Chow or Italian Greyhound.

CIMARRON Title of a gun-slinging Western movie. A bossy pup who feels that your townhouse isn't big enough for both of you could take this name. If you can take him!

CINNAMON An amber-shaded color or a spice derived from fragrant tree bark. A puppy with this name will add a hint of spicy sweetness to your life.

CISCO A term of endearment for San Francisco or just a pup reminiscent of all the city's splendor.

CITRON A tree that bears lemonlike fruit. Bittersweet is your relationship with this new family member.

COLA The main ingredients of this bubbly soft drink are sugar and kola nut extract. An effervescent pup's energetic charades have just taken the place of caffeine for you.

CONGO

COLONEL A military officer who ranks below brigadier general. It's doubtful your pup thinks he ranks below anyone in the family, except maybe the extremely annoyed cat.

COLT Youthful male horse. Perfect name for a budding Great Dane or Mastiff.

COMPADRE Spanish for "friend" or "close companion." *See* AMIGO.

CONFECTION A sweet preparation, just like this puppy.

CONGA An African and Latin American dance having strong drumbeats. This little pup's equivalent might be chasing his or her own tail.

CONGO A jungle region of Africa. Occasional unguided safaris into the wild and dense backyard are taken by this puppy without permission.

CORAZON Spanish for "heart." Warm puppy love only increases with age.

CORDOBA The provincial capital of Andalusia, Spain. Appropriate name for dogs of breeds with Spanish roots or dogs with rich, brown, cordovan coat color.

CORONA A dim halo that surrounds a solar body and can be seen through dim cloud cover, especially around the moon, sun or your somewhat devious little pup.

COUSCOUS This North African dish can be served with meats or vegetables and, in this puppy's case, on his or her kibble.

CRAWDAD *See* SALAMANDER.

CROCUS An annual-blooming tubelike flower. Although this flower's blooms are visible only once a year, your puppy's beauty is discernible year-round.

CUCARACHA Spanish for "cockroach." Good name for a puppy who seems to get into everything.

CUCINA "Kitchen" in Italian. For the dog who always has his or her paw in the cookie jar.

CUERVO This brand of tequila is said to take the hair off your chest. Good name for a Xoloitzcuintli.

CURMUDGEON A finicky, fuddy-duddy of a person . . . or pup.

CURRY A pup named for this common Indian spice will become the spice of your life.

CYPRESS A pine tree with small, compressed needles known to grow in warm climates. Good name for wiry-coated terriers who love to play in the sun.

CZAR "Emperor" or "king." This puppy expects royal treatment. *See* CAESAR *in Chapter 3.*

DAIQUIRI A Cuban cocktail made with rum and citrus juices. A puppy with this name is at times so clumsy that he or she appears "under the influence."

DANK "Thank you" in Dutch. *See* GRAZIE.

DANUBE Named after the Danube River. This name suits dogs with bluish coats: blue Doberman Pinschers, blue Great Danes, Kerry Blue or Bedlington Terriers and Neapolitan Mastiffs.

DELTA This symbol represents the fourth letter of the Greek alphabet. Three puppies may be a charm but the fourth is even better.

DESOTO Resembling the vintage car, clean lines and classic style make this pup an eye-catcher.

DEUCE In many games this throw of dice or game score is thought to bring good luck. Two bright puppy eyes shining up at you will undoubtedly start you on a lucky streak.

DIABLO Spanish for "devil." A name tailor-made for a mischief-making puppy.

DIM SUM Assorted Chinese dumplings and appetizers served mainly for breakfast. Your Chinese Shar-Pei or Pug would happily gobble these up for breakfast, lunch, dinner, snack time or anytime they are within his or her reach.

DINGO This wild Australian dog varies in color from reddish to yellowish brown. This name is suitable for any crazy, seemingly unmanageable pup.

DIVA French for "goddess." Appropriate for any female puppy.

DODGER One who acts deceptively. This probably best describes your troublemaking pup who is the first one gone from the scene of the crime.

DODO The name of this extinct bird, known for its inability to adapt to environmental change and for its flightlessness, is now commonly used as a word of affection for clumsy, oversized creatures, such as your still uncoordinated puppy. *See* KIWI.

DOG *Canis familiaris*, believed to be descended from the wolf, is now a properly domesticated and cared-for pleasure animal. Many words, now part of our everyday language, were derived from this animal's simple name; dog tired, dog-eared, dog biscuit, dog days, dogberry, dogged, dog-catcher, dog-eat-dog, dogface, dogfight, dogfish, doggie bag and doggone, to name just a few. A dog with this name pays tribute to the history of his or her wonderful kind.

DOHENY A popular beach in Southern California. *See* BEACHBABY *in Chapter 2.*

DOLCE and DULCE Respectively, Italian and Spanish for "sweet." Good name for a puppy whose sweet eyes are a match for his or her sweet, playful ways.

DRAMBUIE Much like this liqueur, your puppy with this name warms your heart and lifts your spirits.

DREADNOUGHT A battleship loaded with artillery. This puppy will cause as much mayhem as you let him get away with.

DUBONNET A trade name of an aperitif wine made in France. The difference between the wine and your puppy is that your puppy is sweeter.

DUGONG This aquatic mammal is commonly referred to as a sea cow. Appropriate name for a chubby black Labrador, Doberman Pinscher or Rottweiler.

DURANGO This city in southwest Colorado lies near the New Mexico border. Good name for a bold pup who loves to try new adventures.

EBI Japanese for "shrimp." Probably the smallest of the litter or a dog that is unusually small. Also a good name for a very large dog.

EBONY Meaning "black." Good for a like-colored pup. The name IVORY complements this name when the second dog in your two-dog household is white or cream.

EDELWEISS A small white flower that grows wild in the Bavarian Alps. Good name for a puppy from any of the Toy breeds.

EPCOT Resembling the Florida center filled with imaginative creations, this highly creative and advanced puppy has an intellect that might take keeping up with.

ESPRESSO A strong coffee brewed by steaming rich coffee beans. Too much of this pup at once might tend to make you a little high-strung.

ESPRIT "Spirit." This puppy is not lacking in it.

EUPHRATES A Southwest Asian river. This quick puppy can "flow" through just about any barricade.

EUREKA An expression of triumph on a discovery. Also a way of discerning the authenticity of gold. You hit gold when you found this puppy.

EXETER The hub of many markets lies in this southwest English city, which was rebuilt after brutal World War II bombings. A puppy with this name is often the center of activity.

FABLE A moral tale in which animals often depict characters in order to prove a point. This name is appropriate both for a pup who imparts a sense of moral duty and one who prefers your pillow to his or her doggie bed. Queen Elizabeth used this name for one of her seven Pembroke Welsh Corgis.

FAJITA Chicken or beef is sliced into thin strips and served in a soft tortilla to create this Mexican specialty. This is a good name for a Chihuahua.

FALAFEL This Middle Eastern dish consists mainly of chick-peas and vegetables in a pita. A puppy with this name will probably develop a taste for Middle Eastern food, or simply enjoys any food more than his or her kibble.

FALCON A bird of prey sometimes trained to hunt. The pup so named has grace, energy and boldness.

FANDANGO A colorful, energetic Spanish dance, or perhaps an animated Spaniel.

FANTASIA A composition that does not conform to the standards of structure or induces a fantasy. This pup could inspire even the worst composers.

FAUX PAS A social blunder. Every puppy is bound to have a few . . . or possibly a hundred.

FEDORA The name of this felt hat was used by French playwright Victorien Sardou (1831–1908) as the title for one of his well-known works. This name is appropriate for genteel puppies with smooth, feltlike coats.

FENNEL This edible plant has a flavor similar to licorice. Your puppy might like to gnaw on some.

FENWAY Home park of the Red Sox and known for its large green wall. If you have a Boston Terrier with this name he must be a big-league buddy.

FERREO Spanish for "iron." Good for very muscular or very determined pups.

FIESTA Spanish for "party." This is something you or your pup loves to do.

FIJI This Southwest Pacific country has over eight hundred islands and is a good name for an exotic-looking puppy such as a Basenji or a Chinese Crested.

FIKRI Arabic for "intellectual." Good name for a Doberman Pinscher or German Shepherd Dog.

FLEUR French for "flower," or just a French flower like the French Bulldog, the Papillon or the Petit Basset Griffon Vendeen.

FLORA and FAUNA Plants and animals collectively, especially those that are indigenous to specific areas or time periods. The "Flora" and "Fauna" of your region might have a tendency to become a bit overgrown and unruly if not properly looked after.

FOIE GRAS Goose liver pâté and, much like your eccentric pup, an acquired taste.

FONDUE Cheese, wine and chocolate are the normal delicacies that people dip bread into to create this dish. Your puppy might also choose to dip—sparingly, please—into this delicacy.

FORMOSA An island (now called Taiwan) in the Pacific off the coast of China, as well as an historic Hollywood bar and a beautiful flower. You have a pup who loves to either travel, drink or eat flowers.

FURIOSO Spanish for "having extreme force and energy." This probably describes the way in which your puppy enjoys life.

FUCHSIA An extremely bright purple. Your puppy will stand out in a crowd even more with this name.

GAELIC An old Celtic language, and the name of your puppy of appropriate origin.

GARGOYLE A carving that represents an extremely ugly half human, half animal. The uglier the puppy the more beautiful he or she is to you.

GAZELLE An African or Asian antelope known for its delicate features, slender neck and soft eyes. Good for any equally elegant pooch that fits the same description.

GAZPACHO Spanish chilled soup. Good name for a zesty pup.

GECKO A type of lizard. *See* LIZARD *in Chapter 2.*

GEISHA A Japanese girl who provides entertainment. This pup loves to perform, but expects a treat.

GEMINI This third sign of the zodiac is represented by twins. This twin will always be by your side.

GENESIS The origin of something. You and your pup have just begun a wonderful relationship.

GIMP A limping gait. Good name for a pup with a strut all his or her own.

GIN Alcoholic drink made from rye, grain and juniper berries. Sweet and spirited describe your pup and gin as well.

GINGHAM Dyed cotton fabric that is spun with various colors and patterns. Good name for a uniquely marked puppy of any kind.

GINSENG A root believed to have medicinal and aphrodisiacal qualities. Need more be said about your puppy's ability to make you feel good?

GIRO "Race" in Italian. *See* FLASH *in Chapter 2.*

GIZMO The name of this mechanical gadget is either forgotten or unknown. The madness of puppyhood will not be forgotten, even when your well-behaved senior citizen is resting calmly at your feet.

GNOME A folkloric ageless and mutated dwarf that lives on earth and protects treasures. You now have your own canine protection system.

GORDO Spanish for "fat." *See* FATSO *in Chapter 2.*

GRAZIE Italian for "thank you." Even though your puppy can't speak, he or she expresses this in many ways.

GUAYMAS A port city located in Sonora state, Mexico, known for its striking contrast of dry fertile mountains and luscious blue seas. A pup with this name will add some welcome color and variety to your life.

GUMBO A popular Southern soup. Good name for a Southern puppy such as a Redbone or Treeing Walker Coonhound.

GUMPS An upscale department store in San Francisco, California. This puppy could become accustomed to having all of his or her material desires fulfilled.

GURU In Hinduism this person is acknowledged as a spiritual teacher or leader. You may not be able to teach an old dog new tricks, but maybe you can learn some from him.

GYPSY This name is derived from nomadic people who originally migrated to Europe from Asia. A puppy with this name has an independent, restless nature about him or her.

HACHI-KO This Akita is known in modern Japanese history as a model of fidelity. A statue was erected in his honor in Tokyo, Japan. Like Hachi-Ko's loyalty, your puppy's love for you will be undying.

HAVANA A Cuban city and type of tobacco. Good for any puppy with a deeply-colored, brown coat.

HEAVEN The space or sky that appears to be over Earth. This puppy is living proof that there is Heaven on Earth.

HIPPODROME An open-air stadium originating in ancient Greece. Does your puppy have your home mistaken for one of these?

HOAGIE Meaning "hero" as in "sandwich." All puppies have the potential to be one—the other kind.

HOBBIT A fantasy novel and creature created by J.R.R. Tolkien about a mythological kingdom. Good name for a pup with a fantastic personality.

HOCUS-POCUS Nonsensical words used to play tricks or create illusions. This name probably describes your puppy's interpretation of obedience commands.

HONEYSUCKLE ROSE This multicolored flower is rich in nectar and is as sweet as any adorable puppy.

HOOCH Bootleg liquor named after the Alaskan tribe who made it, supposedly to keep warm on cold nights. An Alaskan Malamute would have gladly served the same purpose.

HOOSIER Nickname for a native or resident of Indiana. Legend has it that the word originated due to its similarity to the sound of wolves howling on cold Midwestern nights. To live up to this name, your puppy will need to be quite vocal in the night hours.

HORS D'OEUVRES Appetizers. Good name for a small, practically bite-sized puppy.

HUGGER-MUGGER Confusion or a muddled state. Your puppy apparently is happiest when wreaking havoc.

ICON A representation, probably of your puppy's beauty.

IDITAROD An Alaskan sled-dog race. Appropriate name for an Alaskan Malamute or Siberian Husky.

INCA A member of an Indian tribe that ruled Peru prior to the Spanish conquest. "Inka" means "ruler" in Spanish. This pup might have a superiority complex around the house and neighborhood, so watch out if he doesn't get his way.

INDIGO A plant that yields a blue dye, ranging from dark blue to grayish purplish blue. *See* BLUE *in Chapter 2.*

INTREPID Courage, endurance and fearlessness are characteristics of this puppy, who might be a serious insurance liability.

IOTA The ninth letter of the Greek alphabet or a very small amount. Good name for a Toy dog.

IRIE "Peace," in Rastafarian, is what this puppy will bring to your life.

IRIS "Rainbow" in Greek and Latin. In Greek mythology Iris was the goddess of the rainbow and messenger of the gods. A multicolored canine who loves to fetch your morning paper could easily wear this name.

ISHTA Arabic for "cream of the crop," or, in doggie terms, "pick of the litter."

J.B. A brand name for a type of whiskey. *See* SCOTCH *in Chapter 2.*

JABBERWOCKY Epitomized by the Lewis Carroll poem with this title, "Jabberwocky" literally is meaningless speech or writing contrived to appear to make sense. A puppy with this name at least pretends to know what is going on.

JACK DANIEL'S A brand name for a type of whiskey and a cute name for a Jack Russell Terrier.

JAG Drunkenness. A young puppy occasionally appears to be under the influence due to his poorly developed coordination.

JAI ALAI A game much like racquetball except played with wicker mallets attached to the hands. This puppy makes a good teammate. He or she loves to chase balls.

JASMINE The scent of this plant is found in its fragrant white flowers. Comical name for a "highly aromatic" puppy.

JAVA A word that has grown in trendy popularity to refer to coffee. A puppy with this name knows how to wake you up in the morning.

JE T'AIME French for "I love you." Puppies say it in many ways, but your puppy's sweet eyes should have a patent on these three words.

JERKY This type of meat is dried and prepared for consumption by curing it. It is a welcomed treat for a dog with the same name or any name.

JUNIPER This bluish gray shrub with prickly growth might resemble the coat of your Border Terrier.

JUPITER As well as being the largest and most massive planet, in Roman mythology this name is given to the supreme god—patron of the Roman state. Good name for a large, massive guard dog.

K-9 Military or police abbreviation for canine. *See* Dog.

KAHLUA A coffee liqueur of dark coloring. Good name for a dog of a similar color.

KAISER Emperor. *See* Caesar *in Chapter 3.*

KALAMAZOO A city in Southwest Michigan, or simply a great-sounding name for a puppy from anywhere.

KALEIDOSCOPE The mirrors and decorations inside this instrument can be moved to produce constantly changing designs. A new and ever-changing perspective of life is seen through the eyes of an ever-growing puppy and his owners.

KARMA In Buddhism and Hinduism, karma is an aura or feeling. You and your puppy might just have the same one. If not, it's bound to develop.

KENTUCKY Good name for a Treeing Walker Coonhound because the breed originated in the Kentucky/Virginia area.

KIELBASA A Polish sausage. See Sausage *in Chapter 2.*

KIKU "Chrysanthemum" in Japanese. Hopefully your puppy will smell as sweet as this flower.

KIMBUNDU A Bantu language of Angola, which means about as much to your puppy as everyday English. Remember, the first word he or she should learn is his or her name, Kimbundu.

KIWI A New Zealand native, this flightless bird is oddly proportioned with stubby legs and a large beak. Does this remind you of your adorably funny puppy?

KLUTZ A clumsy person, or dog. This Yiddish term is often used endearingly, so if this name fits your puppy, don't let him or her hang pictures!

KNAIDEL Little Jewish dumpling, or a puppy who just looks like one.

KOALA This name for the cuddly Aussie marsupial also suits your Australian Terrier, Silky Terrier or any puppy who anxiously wraps around you and clings to your neck.

KOBI "Joy" in Japanese. This puppy will bring much of it to your life.

KONA A relatively large city on the island of Hawaii. Your puppy would love to frolic on the tropical and volcanic beaches nearby with you.

KOOKABURRA A species of kingfisher indigenous to Australia that makes loud, harsh noises, like that of a howling puppy who is spending his or her first night in a new home.

KUDU An African antelope with a brownish, white-striped coat. Good name for a Rhodesian Ridgeback.

KUMA "Bear" in Japanese. *See* BEAR *in Chapter 2.*

LADRON Spanish for "thief." This pup doesn't usually earn his or her treat, he or she steals it.

LAKER A lake-dwelling fish, resembling the trout. This is a good name for any water-loving or basketball aficionado puppy.

LAVENDER The delicate purplish flowers yielded by this plant are commonly used in perfume oils. Good name for a puppy whose sweet scent gives him or her away.

LEXIS Of Greek origin meaning "speech." Appropriate name for a vociferous puppy.

LIEBCHEN "Sweetheart" in German. Good name for dogs of German breeds, but it would suit any sweetheart of a puppy.

LILAC Fragrant purplish, white or pink flowers. Good name for a puppy with a scent all his or her own.

LIMBO A dance in which the participants bend over backwards in order to pass under a pole. Appropriate name for a puppy who has demonstrated unusually agile tendencies.

LIRA Italian currency. You probably paid a pretty penny for this little puppy who is now literally worth his or her weight in gold, at least to you.

LISBON The name of this Portuguese city is a good name for a Portuguese Water Dog.

LOLLY Chiefly British for hard candy and an American shortening of the word "lollipop." This puppy can have a real sweet tooth!

LOTUS Fragrant pinkish flower, resembling in color the nose and paw pads of almost any very young puppy before his or her pigmentation develops.

LUCKY "Good fortune." You are lucky to own this wonderful pup!

MACHETE An immense knife used for slicing vegetation or as a weapon, ... or to cut up prime rib for your puppy's favorite dinner.

MACKEREL Small fish, either Atlantic or Spanish. This puppy is the catch of the day.

MADURO A classic, robust-flavored cigar that comes in dark wrapping. Good name for a similarly shaped, dark-colored Dachshund or Basset Hound.

MAGNA Latin for "great." It is fairly hard to be objective with a name such as this.

MAGNOLIA A family of white, pink, purple, blue or yellow flowers popular in the United States. A colorful personality and sweet-smelling coat are typical of this pup.

MAGNUM A wine bottle that can hold close to two-fifths of a gallon, or an equally large puppy.

MAGPIE An international bird with black, blue or green coloring that is known for its chattering call. This name would suit a chatty puppy.

MAHIMAHI Hawaiian for "dolphin." This intelligent puppy is accustomed to warm and colorful surroundings.

MAI TAI "Good" in Tahitian. Obedience school will help this puppy live up to his or her extremely optimistic name.

MAJESTIC "Dignified" or "grand," like a Great Dane or Afghan Hound.

MAJOR A military officer. Good name for pups who are often called into action on all kinds of campaigns.

MAKO This shark has a weighty body and is known to be dangerous. A pup with this name will command a lot of respect in your neighborhood.

MAMACITA The Spanish term of endearment used for close female friends or relatives. Good name for a Chihuahua.

MAMBA A venomous African tree snake that changes color at will from green to black. An exotic puppy who loves to hide among bushes or trees deserves this name.

MAMBO A Latin American dance that resembles the rumba and cha-cha. This pup might not have all the moves down, but the attitude is there.

MANHATTAN A cocktail made with vermouth and whiskey, named after a borough of New York City. Use this name if you want to give your pup an air of sophistication.

MARASCHINO A type of cherry. A pup with this name will sweeten anyone's life.

MARIACHI A Mexican musical group or a festive puppy who likes to entertain.

MARIGOLD A plant with yellow or orange flowers. Good name for a blond Cocker Spaniel, yellow Labrador or Golden Retriever.

MARLBORO Meaning "rugged" and "having an affinity for the outdoors," as suggested by the popular cigarette ads. Great name for a Saint Bernard or Old English Sheepdog pup.

MARMALADE A fruit preserve. An English favorite, like the Cavalier King Charles Spaniel.

MARQUEE Often found over an entrance to a theater or building, this board is used to draw attention to the building or project an announcement. You can spot this pup from a mile away.

MARTIAN A theoretical creature from the planet Mars. Where you may sometimes think your crazy puppy belongs.

MARTINI Gin or vodka and dry vermouth comprise this drink. This classy pup loves a good party and is a very good mingler.

MATADOR A valiant bullfighter, much like the Bulldog was known to be before the cruel sport of bullbaiting was outlawed in England in 1845. Now this name simply signifies a tenacious little puppy who will chase any- and everything, even a red cape.

MATZO In the Jewish religion, this unleavened bread is eaten during Passover. Good name for a skinny, seemingly flat dog, such as the Whippet.

MAZEL TOV "Congratulations," in Hebrew, are in order for the new four-legged friend joining your family.

MAUI One of the Hawaiian islands, or just a good name for a puppy with the laid-back attitude typical of island people.

MAYA Interpreted in Hinduism as a delusion or a mirage of the mind that signifies the world's end. This pup represents the beginning of your world, but possibly the end of your sofa.

MAYHEM Violent havoc, much like the kind this puppy may wreak on your home if you don't train him or her.

MEADOW An open area of grassland. The smallest plot of grass inspires this pup to burst into an all-out sprint.

MEE-KROB A crunchy Thai dish, mainly consisting of crispy wiry noodles, hence, a good name for dogs of wiry-coated breeds.

MELANGE "A mixture" in French. Definitely a mixed breed!

MENAGE People living unitedly. To say this pup is co-dependent is putting it mildly.

METIS A half-bred or crossbred animal. Appropriate name for a mixed-breed puppy.

MIGNON "Dainty" in French. Cute name for a dog from any of the Toy breeds.

MOHAWK

MING This Chinese dynasty existed from 1368 to 1644. Earlier beliefs and customs were reinstated during this period. Good name for the timeless Pekingese, Shih Tzu or Chow Chow.

MISTLETOE A plant with berries that is often used as a Christmas decoration. This pup works as a good flirting device.

MOET *See* SHRAMSBERG.

MOGUL A small mound on a ski slope, or a small, pudgy pup with a big ego.

MOHAVE An Indian tribe formerly residing near the Colorado River. Appropriate for any dog that resembles the desert-dwelling wolf or fox.

MOHAWK A tribe of Indians who supposedly inhabited the territory of the Mohawk River and made the unique hairstyle of the same name famous. Whimsical name for a Rhodesian Ridgeback or Chinese Crested due to the obvious physical resemblance in the hair.

MOHICAN Another Indian tribe. You might just have the last one.

MON AMI French for "my friend." *See* AMIGO.

MON CHER or MA CHERIE French for "my dear." Your dear puppy's sweetness might inspire you to choose this name.

MONK A male member of a religious group who lives in a monastery with others devoted to the discipline. This would suit a peaceful, serene pup who hardly ever barks.

MONTEGO A popular Jamaican resort. Great name for any dreadlock-bearing puppy like the Komondor or Puli.

MOONSHINE "Nonsensical, meaningless talk." This dog is a real yapper and barks for no apparent reason.

MOSELLE A white wine produced in France near the Moselle River, or a chic name for a *très* chic puppy.

MOUTON A type of sheepskin that resembles beaver or seal. It is appropriate for Bedlington Terriers due to their characteristic lamblike appearance.

MULBERRY Grayish to dark purple. Good for like-colored and equally sweet puppies like the Kerry Blue Terrier or a blue or silver Poodle.

MUSTANG Descended from horses imported by the Spaniards, this wild horse now lives on the open ranges of North America. This name would suit a free spirit even if his domain was no greater than the backyard.

MYTH An imaginary or fictitious belief, story, person or thing, also the name of one of Queen Elizabeth's seven Pembroke Welsh Corgis.

NACHO A triangular crunchy tortilla often topped with various Mexican condiments. This pup might earn his name by diving into a bag of these munchies.

NAPA A popular wine-making region in Northern California, or maybe a grape-loving pup living there.

NAPPY British for an infant's diaper. You can only wish they made them for this little pup.

NAVAJO A tribe of Indians presently occupying a large reservation in Arizona, New Mexico and Utah. This territorial puppy takes up a lot of room.

NAVAR Navigation by means of radar. This pup has a very keen sense of direction. *See* RADAR *in Chapter 2.*

NEPTUNE Discovered by Galileo, this planet has gusting winds and a large dark spot. Good name for a spotted puppy with a breezy personality.

NEUTRON An electrically neutral particle, or your minuscule but powerful puppy.

NEWSPRINT Cheap, thin paper, used primarily for printing newspaper, . . . and housebreaking.

NINJA A Japanese warrior who is well trained in martial arts and the skillful use of weaponry. Good name for a puppy with protective instincts.

NOEL A Christmas song, or another name for Christmas itself. Suitable for a puppy born or given to you on such a momentous day.

NOISETTE "Little nut" in French. Your puppy's head might at times seem to be filled with little nuts instead of brains.

NOSFERATU Vampire. Good name for a puppy that focuses on nuzzling your neck.

NOVA A new star that grows in luminosity, then returns to its earlier lightness. To you, this puppy will always shine on brighter than the rest.

NOVELLA A short novel. Your puppy's whining antics are an easy read.

NUDGE Yiddish for "a pest, nag or bother." You couldn't agree more when your loving puppy persists in dropping slobber-covered tennis balls in your lap.

NUTMEG This fragrant seed ranges in color from dingy to dark brown and is widely used as a spice. Good for like-colored puppies.

NYMPH In Greek and Roman mythology, this was supposedly one of many female, animal-like spirits that represented sectors of nature such as woodlands and water. Also an incredibly attractive girl or, in your case, puppy.

ODYSSEY Stemming from Homer's epic poem, this word represents an adventurous, lingering voyage that might typify your puppy's evening walks.

OINK The natural grunting sounds of a hog, or your short-nosed pup.

OKRA This plant has pods that are an ingredient in gumbo soup, and, if your puppy gets his or her way, over kibble.

OMEGA The last letter of the Greek alphabet. A cute name for the last pick of the litter.

ONOMATOPOEIA If you could spell some of the noises this puppy makes you could write an entirely new dictionary.

ONYX A type of gemstone that is found in various colored bands and is used significantly in cameos. Good for spotted, streaked or brindled pups.

OPAL An iridescent mineral and gem. Also a name commonly given to babies in the early decades of the twentieth century, about the same time the Boston Terrier gained popularity. Your Boston might like it.

OUIJA The trademark name of a board with the alphabet and other symbols on it that supposedly relays spiritualistic messages to the user. You never know when this clairvoyant puppy might be telling you something, so always take heed of his or her clues.

OUTLAW A fugitive or sociopathic person or animal. Comical name for a very docile puppy.

PACHYDERM A large, thick-skinned mammal such as a rhinoceros or elephant. A Great Dane, Mastiff, Rottweiler or Saint Bernard could take this name.

PADUA A northeastern Italian city located west of Venice. This puppy's taste in fine food might be easy to satisfy, but fine wine and women are another story.

PAGAN A person who fails to adhere to any religion and relishes forbidden pleasures and material possessions. You will have to watch this especially demanding puppy quite closely.

PAGODA A Far Eastern structure used especially by Buddhists as a religious memorial. An equally stoic and traditional-looking puppy whose breed originated in China deserves this name, possibly a Chow Chow or Chinese Shar-Pei.

PALOMINO A showy-looking horse with a golden or tan coat and a white mane and tail. Good name for a Golden Retriever or yellow Labrador.

PANAMA This Central American country links North and South America. Good name for a pup who is often the center of attention.

PANDORA Pandora, the first woman to exist according to Greek mythology, out of curiosity opened a box known by the same name and set free the evils of the world. You had no idea what you were getting into with this lovable puppy.

PAPILLON French for "butterfly." Good name for a Papillon or any puppy with really big ears.

PAPOOSE An Indian baby, or your little puppy.

PAPRIKA A vivid reddish orange color and a seasoning created by crushing dried red peppers. Widely used in Hungarian cooking, it makes a good name for a Vizsla or other like-colored dogs.

PAPU "Grandpa" in Greek. A puppy with this name will always be there when you need him.

PAPYRUS A paper made from the papyrus reed, used in antiquity as the first known writing material. And your puppy might be the first to bear this innovative name.

PAZZO Italian for "crazy." This puppy enjoys chasing shadows and invisible ghosts.

PENNE Tubular pasta. Cute name for a Basset Hound or Dachshund, who, according to author and poet Robert Benchley, "are ideal dogs for small children, as they are already stretched and pulled to such a length that the child cannot do much harm one way or the other."

PERIWINKLE Like this blue- and white-flowered plant cultivated for ground cover, your huge-pawed puppy will never seem to stop growing.

PERNOD Much like the French licorice-flavored aperitif, this pup gives a sweet impression.

PERRO "Dog" in Spanish. *See* Dog.

PESO "The weight of something" in Spanish. Good name for a Chihuahua or other Toy dog.

PETIT ANGE French for "little angel." Much like the little pup who insists the cat did it.

PETUNIA The colors of this flower range from white to purple to dark purple. However, they don't get any prettier or more exotic than your canine flower with this name.

PEYOTE A drug known to induce hallucinations. An overly imaginative pup deserves this name.

PHARAOH The title given to an ancient Egyptian king. Good name for a Pharaoh Hound.

PHAROS An island near Alexandria, Egypt, famous for its ancient lighthouse. Also the name of one of Queen Elizabeth's seven Pembroke Welsh Corgis.

PHOENIX Legend has it that this bird lived for five hundred years, then burned and was reborn from its own ashes. This would be a super name for any "recycled" rescue or pound adoptee.

PIAZZA These public squares in Italian towns always have a clown. You now have yours.

PICCOLO A very small flute pitched higher than a regular one. The word is also used in Italian to mean "small." This name accurately describes any Toy or small-breed pup, especially a rather noisy one.

PIEDMONT Situated and resting near the base of a mountain range. This dog is large and easygoing.

PIGGY A mammal of the Suidae family, possessing short legs, pointed hoofs, prickly hair and a snout used for rooting. *See* BACON *in Chapter 2.*

PINTO An irregularly marked horse descended from similar Spanish horses. Good also for spotted, streaked, piebald or brindle-colored puppies.

PIROUETTE A balletic turn accomplished by balancing one's weight and spinning on the tip of the toe or ball of the foot, or a pup whose agility and grace never cease to amaze you.

PIZZAZZ Gusto, enthusiasm and flair are just a few of this energetic pup's qualities.

POCO "Small quantity" in Spanish. Good name for a dog from one of the miniature or Toy breeds.

POLTERGEIST A clamorous ghost, or puppy, accustomed to pulling harmless pranks.

POOH-BAH A conceited official who presides over numerous positions, but fails to perform their duties. This pup is all bark and no bite.

POTPOURRI A mixture or collection of various elements. And a great name for a dog of unknown origin.

POUILLY-FUISSÉ A dry white wine. *See* CHABLIS *in Chapter 2.*

PRESTO Music in rapid tempo. Also, Italian for "suddenly, at once." This might characterize the way your pup runs when he or she hears dinner being served.

PRIMO "First" in Spanish. This name could further spoil a pup who already thinks he should be first in line for everything.

PRINCE A hereditary ruler. An outstanding man in a group or class, or just your knight in shining fur.

PROTON The positively charged portion of an atom. Also a good name for a compact but powerful pup.

PUPA "Female doll" in Italian. And the newest little doll in your family.

RASTA

PYGMY In Greek mythology, an unusually small race of dwarfs. It might be fun to watch your Great Dane, Saint Bernard or Mastiff grow out of this name. But it is more appropriate for seemingly dwarfed breeds like Dachshunds or Welsh Corgis.

QUASI "Almost" in Italian. For the dog who's almost never obedient.

QUEENY A woman ruler, having authority over a particular domain. This name is appropriate for a high-maintenance puppy with very expensive taste in toys and food.

RAGTIME A jazz style composed of an irregular rhythm combined with a steady accompaniment. This steady accompaniment might be characterized by this puppy's constant tail wagging.

RAJAH An Indian prince or emperor. *See* PRINCE.

RASTA Short for "Rastafarian" (Rastafarianism). A devout Jamaican group whose people praise Haile Selassie, originally from Ethiopia. Good name for breeds having corded coats or dreadlocks, such as the Komondor and Puli.

RAZZMATAZZ Showy actions performed with the intention of creating confusion. A puppy who has added a bit of bewilderment to your household deserves this name.

REEF A formation of sand, sharp rocks or coral close to the surface of a body of water. This is one sharp puppy.

REGALO "Present" in Spanish. This gift of a puppy will forever keep on giving.

REM An acronym for "Rapid Eye Movement." Sporadic, quick and short-lived describe both this period of sleep and your puppy's attention span.

RENEGADE One who challenges normal standards of behavior. Appropriate for a puppy who likes to do things his or her own way. *See* REBEL *in Chapter 2.*

RENO A gambling city in Nevada, or just a pup you took a chance on that turned into a winner.

RHODES An eastern Greek island known for its school of rhetoric. This yappy puppy must be one of its star pupils.

RHONE A river cutting through Switzerland and France. Good for sophisticated pups of breeds from this region.

RICHES Considerable wealth and possessions, like your priceless new friend.

RICOCHET To rebound. This high-strung puppy is usually bouncing off your walls.

RICOTTA This white, creamy cheese originated in Italy, and would make a tasty name for any white dog.

RIO Spanish for "large river" or your flamboyantly exotic puppy who promises to grow into this name.

ROCCA A nut- and chocolate-covered candy. A sweet treat like your puppy.

ROCOCO A French eighteenth-century artistic style known for its whimsical and complicated decoration. Good name for a flamboyant puppy who incessantly tries to up-stage you.

ROGUE A playful prankster or rascal. This puppy might need more discipline than others if he or she is half as bad as this name indicates.

ROJO "Red" in Spanish. *See* RED *in Chapter 2.*

ROMA The capital city of Italy. *See* PADUA.

ROOKIE An inexperienced player or newcomer. Appropriate name for a gutsy puppy who could use a little more training.

ROT "Red" in German. *See* RED *in Chapter 2.*

RUBY A precious, deep red stone. Pretty name for puppies with shiny red coats.

SABER A dangerous fighting sword, this is a good name for a pup who promises to be a protector.

SABER-TOOTH Derived from a species of extinct cat; a puppy with this name will probably require a lot of chew toys.

SABLE A Russian member of the weasel family famous for its soft, dark fur. Good name for puppy with a similar coat, such as a black or chocolate Labrador.

SAFARI A journey designed for exploration or hunting. Long, taxing walks are this pup's favorite pastime.

SAFFRON Vivid yellow to orange, much like the coat of a Golden Retriever or yellow Labrador.

SAGE An experienced, wise and respected person. This little puppy has a mind all his or her own.

SAHARA The North African desert. This heat-tolerant puppy loves to take afternoon naps in the sun.

SALAMANDER (MANDY) Small lizard-like amphibian with four weak and undeveloped legs. This puppy really depends on you.

SAMBUCA Like the Italian licorice-flavored liqueur, this pup warms your heart and lifts your spirits.

SAMURAI A highly skilled Japanese warrior. This pup is well equipped to protect you.

SANGRIA A Spanish wine cooler made of red wine, sugar, fruit juice and seltzer. Quite a mixture. This sweet puppy is definitely an eclectic blend.

SANTO "Saint" in Spanish; however, this name can apply to the most devilish of puppies.

SASHIMI Raw fish, traditionally served as a Japanese entrée. Good name for an Akita or Shiba Inu.

SATAY A Thai dish consisting of skewered meat, and a comically intimidating name for any puppy.

SAVERNAKE This English forest, located just outside London, is the perfect setting for a happy puppy so named to romp in.

SAVOY The ruling dynasty of Sardinia, Italy, and Spain. A good name for the slightly overterritorial puppy.

SCAMPI A popular shrimp dish. If this is a favorite of yours, your new puppy of the same name may have a personality to savor.

SCHATZIE "Little treasure" or "little sweetheart" in German. Perfectly suits any puppy.

SCHNAPPS Strong liquor, or an active pup. Good name for a Boxer or any size Schnauzer.

SCHNOOK A dense person. Obedience training will probably require some special tutoring for him or her.

SCHOONER A multi-sailed ship, or a large beer glass, or just your large puppy.

SCOOTER A scientific nickname for the white cloud around Neptune, or your cloudlike Bichon Frise, Samoyed or West Highland White Terrier.

SCORPIO The eighth sign of the zodiac. Although this puppy might be a bit self-centered and stubborn, he or she compensates by being uncomplaining and trusting.

SEA DOG A very experienced sailor. You might want to consider a house by the beach for this pup.

SENECA North American Indians who formerly inhabited New York State. Good for pups that are happiest living close to nature.

SERA Italian for "night." Good for any pup with a coat as black as night.

SERENDIPITY The ability to make unplanned discoveries. This pup occasionally makes your favorite shoes or tie disappear and reappear.

SERENGETI A North Tanzanian animal reserve. Wonderful name for a Basenji or Rhodesian Ridgeback.

SERGEANT A military officer often elected to command troops. A puppy deserving of this name might have you rethink who's walking who.

SEYCHELLES An island chain off the eastern coast of Kenya that went untouched by tourists for years. This puppy is a natural beauty.

SHAH The Iranian head of state. This pup will carry some weight in your household.

SHALIMAR Gardens that remained from the Mongol era, which your puppy could undoubtedly demolish with pleasure and efficiency.

SHANGRI-LA A beautiful, almost perfect, imaginary haven. This place for your puppy is underneath your down comforter.

SHAWNEE A North American Indian tribe, and early inhabitants of Tennessee. Good name for a Treeing Walker Coonhound or any other rugged outdoor dog.

SHEER "Poem" or "song" in Hebrew. Good name for the puppy with much rhyme or reason.

SHERWOOD A royal forest in Nottingham, England, and home of the legendary hero Robin Hood. This pup takes from the large, bullying pups and gives to the meek, small ones.

SHIKSA Yiddish word used to describe a non-Jewish girl. However, your nondenominational pup won't care either way.

SHIITAKE A type of gourmet mushroom. Good name for a puppy such as the Chinese Shar-Pei whose wrinkled appearance brings to mind a fusty little mushroom.

SHOGUN Japanese military leader who until 1868 exercised complete rule. Good name for a puppy of Japanese origin, such as the Akita or Shiba Inu.

SHRAMSBERG A California vineyard known for its fine champagnes. An effervescent personality is what the pup with this name will be known for.

SHRIMP A small, usually pinkish edible crustacean. Good for tiny dogs or dogs too big for the name.

SICILIANO A native of Sicily. This pup is known to have friends in high places.

SIENNA A deep reddish orange. *See* Paprika.

SIERRA A mountain range known for its harshness and jagged contours. An equally rugged Alaskan Malamute, Great Pyrenees or Saint Bernard fits this name.

SMORES Marshmallows and chocolate roasted between graham crackers, a favorite treat, just like your puppy.

SNOOKER Like the pocket billiard game that uses primarily red balls, this pup is difficult to master.

SOLEIL French for "sun." This name is appropriate for the canine sunshine of your life.

SONATA Like this musical composition that varies in pitch, mood and tempo, this moody pup can be challenging to follow.

SOONER Slang for a resident of Oklahoma. You're lucky this pup has taken up residence in your home.

SOUEEE A call for pigs. Good name for your potbellied pup.

SOURDOUGH Slang for an old-time settler or prospector. This curious puppy is a genuine explorer.

SPAGO A single piece of spaghetti. This would make a good name for a long-bodied, thin dog.

SPHINX A figure from Egyptian and Greek mythology that supposedly possessed the body of a lion and head of a human. Good name for a Pharaoh Hound.

SPUTNIK This word literally means a "traveling partner," however it has also become a household term due to the satellite launched into space by the USSR. This intelligent puppy will forever be by your side.

STETSON A trademark name for a wide-brimmed hat. This highfalutin puppy has a little bit of country in him- or herself.

STREGA "Witch" in Italian. Good name for any female puppy who doesn't always listen to your commands.

SUKIYAKI A Japanese beef entrée soaked in soy sauce and sake. Good name for an Akita or Shiba Inu.

SULFUR Like the nonmetallic element used to make gunpowder, this puppy's explosive personality ignites a playfulness in others.

SULTAN A ruler, especially of a Moslem country. This stoic puppy will command equal if not greater respect than his or her namesake.

SUMO Japanese wrestling in which participants attempt to force each other out of bounds. The larger the wrestler, the better chance he has of winning. Any chubby puppy who likes to throw his or her weight around would carry this name well.

SUNI A tribal name for a small African antelope. Good name for a Basenji.

SUSSUDIO Named after this Phil Collins song, a puppy with this name probably has good timing. *See* BRIT *in Chapter 2.*

SWAMI A Hindu teacher, lord and mystic. Good name for a Japanese Chin, Lhasa Apso or Shih Tzu.

T-BONE A beefsteak from the section of the loin having the T-shaped bone. This pup earned his name due either to his love for T-bones or his yummy-looking legs. *See* PORKCHOP *in Chapter 2.*

TABRIZ An area of Iran (formerly Persia) and a rug style, or just an affinity for wetting it.

TALISMAN A good luck charm used to cast away evil spirits. Petting and rubbing this pup are suggested.

TANG A pungent taste or flavor. There is nothing this unscrutinizing pup won't eat.

TANKA A Japanese poem. This one is a real work of art.

TAO Chinese for "path." This puppy knows the way to your heart.

TAOS A resort north of New Mexico.

TARO A plant found in tropical climates with characteristically large leaves. Resembling this plant, your exotic puppy could have big ears.

TARTINE French for "a little piece of buttered toast," like what your puppy is always begging for.

TARTUFFE This play by Molière (1622–1673) evolves around a hypocritical character. This is like a puppy who cries to get up on the bed, then wets it once he is there.

TEAL A greenish blue color, typical of a small wild duck, like the coat of the blue Doberman Pinscher, Kerry Blue Terrier and Neapolitan Mastiff.

TEMPEST A strong storm often including wind, rain, snow or hail, which probably resembles your puppy if deprived of his or her nap.

TEQUILA A Central American or Mexican liquor. It is said this liquor will take the hair off your chest; case in point, the Mexican Hairless, or Chinese Crested.

TEXAS Everyone loves Texas. Things are said to be preferred big there, hence, it's a good name for dogs from naturally large breeds like the Great Dane.

TI AMO Italian for "I love you." Treat this pup to your love and you'll never regret it. *See* JE T'AIME.

TIARA An ornate jeweled crown. An elegant pup who loves formal occasions would wear this name well.

TITAN An extremely strong, large being. This name is appropriate for all the powerful, imposing breeds and is fun for all the "little guys."

TITIAN An orangish brown. *See* PAPRIKA.

TOFU Bean curd, oddly enough, might be this vegetarian pup's favorite treat.

TOPAZ A light yellow type of quartz. Good for breeds with this coloring.

TOREADOR *See* MATADOR.

TORO "Bull" in Spanish or just Bulldog, Bull Terrier or Bullmastiff to you.

TORTS Wicked acts, such as those committed by your mischievous puppy, have earned him this name.

TOVA "Good" in Hebrew. It takes a very special puppy to earn this incredibly optimistic name.

TRILOGY A sequence of three works that together create one theme. Appropriate name for the third dog of the family, who will finally make your household complete.

TRINKET A miniature decorative adornment, like your Yorkshire Terrier, Miniature Pinscher or other little gem.

TROUT Greek for "to gnaw," and Latin for "a fish with sharp teeth." Therefore, any slippery, chew-happy, water-loving puppy could appropriately be named this.

TRYST French for "lovers' rendezvous," which in the case of your puppy is occasionally held on your new down comforter.

TSUNAMI An enormous tidal wave. A pup with this name will definitely make waves in your home.

TULIP A multicolored and flashy flower. Sounds like this pup would look good wearing a bow.

TUMBLEWEED A plant native to dry regions and often found blowing about in the wind, or a puppy who is so small and wiry that you should be careful she doesn't blow away.

TUNDRA A barren Arctic landscape. Stomping grounds for rugged pups such as the Alaskan Malamute, Samoyed and Siberian Husky.

TYPHOON *See* HURRICANE *in Chapter 2.*

UGLY-BUGLY The English version of "ugly." Cute name for dogs deemed by most to be attractive only on the inside.

URANUS The seventh planet. Little is known about this mysterious blue-green planet except that it has a strangely tilted rotational axis. Good name for an equally mysterious puppy with an offbeat balance.

UTOPIA A place of illusory and ideal perfection. This must be where your angelic pup originated.

VACA Spanish for "cow." Appropriate name for a slow-moving puppy whose coat resembles that of a cow. He or she probably even has little, floppy ears.

VAQUERO Spanish for "cowboy or herdsman." Good name for a little pup who likes to chase things bigger than himself.

VERONA A city in northeastern Italy. This pup's name reflects your taste for the finer things in life.

VICHYSSOISE This cold potato soup would please your puppy atop his or her kibble.

VIVA Italian for "long life." Good name for a puppy who gets excited over just about anything.

VOODOO A superstitious type of black magic. Putting needles through dolls is mild compared to how this pup mangles them. It is enough to make any voodoo believer jumpy.

WALRUS An aquatic mammal related to the seals, it has long tusks, wrinkled skin and a wise expression. A good name for your "wiseacre" pup.

WASABE Like this green, very hot condiment that accompanies sushi, this puppy is potent even in small doses.

WELLINGTON Calling this pup's name might create a stir at the park, whether he's named for your boots, a gourmet beef dish or the English Duke who defeated Napoleon at the Battle of Waterloo.

WHISKEY See SCOTCH in Chapter 2.

WILLOW "Grace," or graceful, is what your Afghan Hound or Saluki pup will grow into.

WITCH See STREGA.

WONTON A Chinese pork-filled dumpling. Remind you of a Chinese Shar-Pei?

XANADU A fictitious location of utopian beauty. See UTOPIA.

YAYA "Grandma" (spelled phonetically) in Greek. See BABUSHKA.

YAMASEE An Indian tribe. A renegade pup with this name brings to mind the courage of these people.

YORGY The Greek form of "little George." Good name for any nice dog you can cozy up to, especially your Yorkshire Terrier.

YOSEMITE A national park in central Calfornia. To say this pup is wild about the outdoors is an understatement.

YUKON A river flowing through Canada and Alaska. Good name for pups of sled dog breeds, such as the Alaskan Malamute, Samoyed and Siberian Husky.

YULE Christmas or the celebration of it. Great for a puppy given and received on Christmas. This one is cause for much celebration.

YUMA An Arizona town, or a sexy name for a sassy pup.

ZAIRE An East African country. Good name for a Rhodesian Ridgeback.

ZEBU An unusual breed of ox. *See Ox in Chapter 2.*

ZEKE "Spark" in Hebrew is a clue to what this pup can do for your life-style.

ZEPHYR Like a soft breeze, this pup's calm demeanor is refreshing.

ZULU A southeast African member of a particular Bantu nation. This puppy is both primitive and spiritual.

ZUNI A North American Indian tribe. This puppy does not care if he lives in a pueblo, doghouse or mansion as long as he is with you.

2

Tall Tails

T HE NAMES in this chapter appeal to adults and children alike. They were compiled in response to parents' need to ooh, aah and coo into their new puppies' ears. Some are unique names, with anecdotal stories describing their origin or physical characteristics associated with a dog who would wear such a name. Others stem from words or sounds that simply, easily and humorously roll off the tongue.

A CAPPELLA Without you this puppy would be all alone.

ABRACADABRA Bringing this puppy home has just added a bit of magic to your life.

ACE is wild. Which about sums up this pup.

ACTION Good name for a puppy in constant motion. The name becomes increasingly comical with age, when many dogs become couch potatoes.

ADMIRAL A lover of the high seas. This was the name of the first Irish Setter registered in the United States, in 1878.

AFFINITY A strong liking for just about anything could earn a puppy this name: toys, rawhide, sofas, affection, even cats.

ALPINE A mountain dog, like the Bernese Mountain Dog, Great Pyrenees or Saint Bernard.

AMARETTO A touch of sweet flavoring has been added to your life.

AMBASSADOR A puppy with this name is able to negotiate as many treats as he or she wants.

AMETHYST A soothing puppy with healing qualities.

AMPERSAND This new addition will work as a connecting force in the family.

ANGEL This starry-eyed, affectionate puppy may stretch your limits if you allow him or her to destroy your home.

ANIMAL Contrary to his or her name, your puppy will probably evolve into a well-mannered and civilized member of your family.

APPRENTICE Good listening and quick learning are traits that make this name appropriate for this pooch.

ASHES Ashes to ashes, dust to dust, this puppy will destroy your house; it's obedience training or bust.

ASIA Probably a well-traveled pup. Good name for Akitas, Chinese Shar-Peis, Lhasa Apsos, Shih Tzus or any other breed originating in the Orient.

ASPHALT One look at this roadside puppy and you knew he was worth stopping for.

ASSET A welcomed addition to your life.

ASYLUM At times this puppy's behavior makes you wonder if he or she should be committed. But by the end of puppyhood you will be the one who needs to get away.

ATOM This little source of energy is practically indivisible from you. Good name for a small dog.

AUDACITY A shameless, fearless pooch.

AUDITOR Don't think this contemplative baby is just watching the world go by. He's taking notes.

AUSSIE Although frequently exiled to the backyard due to his outspokenness and attitude, this pooch is as friendly as his homeland. Good name for an Australian Cattle Dog or a Silky Terrier.

AUTOBAHN The fastest-moving puppy in the world, or so he seems. Great name for a German Shepherd Dog or Doberman Pinscher.

AUTUMN By Christmas this puppy might even be housebroken.

AVALANCHE A large mass of a dog who can make more of a mess than is believable.

B.B. Beautiful Baby.

BABA Good name for puppies who look like little lambs: Bedlington Terriers, Bichon Frises, Clumber Spaniels, Maltese and white Poodles.

BABY (also BABY-DOLL or BABYKINS) Particularly good name for extremely large breeds: Great Danes, Mastiffs, Newfoundlands, Rottweilers and Saint Bernards.

BABY-FACE A face only a mother could love, such as that of a Bulldog, Boston Terrier, Chinese Shar-Pei or Pug.

BACON Some breeds possessing Suidae qualities such as legs the shape of porkchops and rooting tendencies are occasionally likened to pigs. Good for an American Staffordshire Terrier, Bulldog, Boston Terrier, Dachshund, Pug or any mud-loving puppy.

BADGER This pup doesn't bother earning his or her treat but instead badgers you for it.

BAHAMA MAMA This puppy will be very disappointed if you leave her when you go on vacation.

BALDY Dogs should have hair. Good name for a Xoloitzcuintli.

BALLERINA This puppy's grace will never cease to astound you. With clumsy pirouettes and overextended leaps she can singlehandedly ruin your home.

BAMBOOZLER How many treats will you give to this puppy?

BANDANNA A truly spoiled puppy has his or her bandanna changed daily to match Mommy's attire.

BANDIT One who tries to make off with the bacon.

BANJO Good name for a musically inclined hound who loves to romp in the hay.

BANNER Her name says it all. You will want to show this baby off to the whole neighborhood.

BANSHEE We suggest taking this pup's wails seriously.

BARBARIAN Eating off the floor and sleeping in the mud are just a couple of this puppy's primitive tendencies.

BARFLY Suitable for older, more seasoned dogs.

BASS A real catch!

BAYOU Good name for a bluish-colored dog. *See* BLUE.

BAZOOKA Be careful—this pup is loaded and ready to fire, and you never know what the damage will be.

BEACHBABY For a puppy who can't stay away from the sand and salt.

BEACHCOMBER *See* BEACHBABY.

BEAMER You could swear this puppy is smiling at you.

BEANS Don't underestimate this one. His magical abilities make him a jack-of-all-trades.

BEAR Hibernation is a favorite pastime. Good name for breeds that resemble bear cubs as puppies: Akitas, Chow Chows and Great Pyrenees.

BEARLOCK HOLMES It is amazing what this puppy can snoop out.

BEAUTY Could "beast" be more appropriate for your puppy?

BEEPER Good name for a dog who always comes when he or she is called.

BEGONIA A budding puppy deserves this flowering name.

BELLBOY More than happy to satisfy every one of your needs. Just don't forget to tip him.

BERBER Your puppy might earn this name by costing you your living room carpet, or maybe you recarpeted just for him.

BEWITCHED by this puppy's cuteness.

BIG BOY Leader of the pack.

BIGFOOT Little paws leave big imprints.

BIG TIME This showboat of a puppy has quite a big chip on his or her shoulder.

BIKER *See* HARLEY.

BIMBO Definitely a blond—Cocker Spaniel, Soft Coated Wheaten Terrier, yellow Labrador or Golden Retriever; it's your call.

BINGO A big hit with the older folks, just like the Boston Terrier and Miniature or Toy Poodle.

BIRDY Good name for any hunting dog: Pointers, Retrievers, Setters, Spaniels, Weimaraners, Wirehaired Pointing Griffons, Vizslas and even Poodles.

BISHOP An esteemed leader.

BITS Desperately seeking KIBBLES.

BIZZY Keeping this curious little busybody entertained is always a pleasure.

BLACKBIRD Good for black pups who are under the delusion that they can fly.

BLACKIE Time-tested name for any black dog—purebred or mix.

BLACKJACK Your puppy is a full hand to deal with.

BLAZE A dog that aimlessly beelines around the backyard, blazing the trail as well as the flower bed.

BIGFOOT

BOMBSHELL

BLIMP This puppy might be a little too round for his or her own good.

BLONDIE Ask your yellow Labrador if blonds have more fun.

BLOSSOM For a puppy who is growing and blooming before your very eyes.

BLOTTO A little hair of the dog that bit you.

BLUBBER Good name for any chubby little pup.

BLUE Good name for a dog whose coat has a hint of blue in it: blue Doberman Pinschers, blue Great Danes, Kerry Blue Terriers, blue Neapolitan Mastiffs and blue Chow Chows all qualify.

BLUEBERRY See BLUE.

BLUEPRINT Good name for the second dog of the house if he or she is of the same breed as the first.

BLUES This puppy might "sing" a little more than you like.

BLUNDER Mistakes have been happening all too often since this puppy moved in. This was the name of the first Beagle registered with the AKC, in 1885.

BODACIOUS See BOMBSHELL.

BOJANGLES A singing gypsy of a puppy with bells on his collar, which make it easier for the cat of the household to hear him or her coming.

BOLERO Good name for any active dog who anxiously dances around you for attention.

BOLLA Suave to say the least!

BOLOGNA This dog's favorite line is "the cat did it."

BOMBSHELL Watch out, all you perfect tens, now you've got some competition.

BONBON Good name for a Poodle.

BONES This puppy isn't picky, but make sure to keep this as his name and not as part of his diet.

BONFIRE Don't spoil him or her too much. This vain pup will have you convinced that he is both Master of the Universe and of your home.

BONGO The noise this puppy makes!

BOOBER It's nice to let your children name the puppy.

BOOGABOO An original name, to say the most.

BOGEYMAN No bogeyman could get near you with this protective pup around.

BOOGIE-WOOGIE Beagle Boy of Company B.

BOOKER To protect, serve and honor. Perfect for a German Shepherd Dog or Doberman Pinscher.

BOOKIE Your bet should always be on this puppy. He's a sure thing.

BOOM-BOOM Not a name for a quiet, calm pup.

BOOMER Short for "boomerang." The most loyal pup of all. This one will always come back.

BOOTS For a dog whose paws look more like boots due to their coloration. These boots were made for walkin', and they will appreciate every walk you take them on.

BOOZER This puppy hasn't quite developed enough co-ordination to act sober.

BOSS Good name for a pup who already runs the house-hold.

BOSSMAN *See* HONCHO.

BOUNCER Be sure to tell friends that small bribes might avoid a protective once-over from this dog.

BOUQUET Springtime freshness will abound in your house with the arrival of this beautiful bouquet. If you like the fragrance of clean dogs and sweet puppy breath.

BOY Frogs and snails and puppy dog tails are what this little puppy is made of.

BOZO This shameless ham is quite often a crowd pleaser.

BRAIN Comical name for a puppy who consistently fails to respond to his or her name or who flunked obedience training, but more appropriate for a Doberman Pinscher, German Shepherd Dog or Poodle.

BRAINCHILD Extremely intelligent. This puppy is always trying to pull the wool over your eyes.

BRAINDEAD An obedience school flunky, but he or she is still an A-plus student to you.

BRANDY This amber-colored bundle of warm, soothing spirit might soon take the place of your nightcap. Good name for an Irish Setter.

BRANDYWINE *See* Brandy.

BRASSY This puppy's bark has a resonance all its own.

BRAT Spoiling this dog might just make her live up to her name, especially for intelligent canines who test their limits.

BRATWURST (BRAUTTY) Resembling the tasty popular sausage, this name works for all short-haired dogs who wiggle into sausage shapes or who literally look like sausages. Especially good name for a Dachshund.

BRAVO A little bit of enthusiasm will spark performance after performance from this puppy.

BREW No one really knows what makes up this one-of-a-kind pup.

BREWSKY A soothing companion for those Sunday afternoon sporting events.

BRIT Good name for a Brittany, or a puppy from a British breed such as the Bulldog, English Toy Spaniel or Mastiff.

BROADWAY You hit the big time with this puppy.

BRONCO A seemingly untameable bucking Great Dane or Mastiff pup who promises to grow as big as a horse.

BROUHAHA What a ruckus this puppy creates.

BROWN SUGAR A necessary ingredient in all kitchens, . . . living rooms, bedrooms, dining rooms . . .

BROWNIE *See* CHOCOLATE.

BRUIN *See* BEAR.

BUBBA Good name for a Bulldog.

BUBBLES You won't be able to keep this pup out of the tub. Appropriate name for water-loving breeds, such as Labradors, Newfoundlands and Poodles.

BUCCANEER This puppy lives for adventure and has little to no regard for his or her safety in its pursuit.

BUCKAROO A real cowboy of a puppy.

BUCKSHOT Good companion for any hunting aficionado.

BRATWURST

BUG

BUDDY The stereotypical house dog. He's everybuddy's best friend.

BUFFOON Clumsy puppy antics might make him appear a bit slow-witted, but this baby will grow into his gracefulness.

BUFFY Why do so many people name their dogs this?

BUG This puppy always seems to be swarming around you. Good name for small dogs with large eyes and very short faces: Boston Terriers, Brussels Griffons, English Toy Spaniels, Japanese Chins, Pekingese, Pugs and Shih Tzus.

BUGINARUG This little cuddling puppy likes nothing better than snuggling up in your blankets.

BUGTUSSIE This dog must, in some way, resemble a bug. *See* BUG.

BUICK American-made, just like the Boston Terrier.

BULLET An aerodynamic dog whose searing speed leaves others in the dust. Good name for a Bull Terrier.

BULLFACE Good name for a Bulldog or Boxer.

BULLION This puppy is worth his or her weight in gold.

BUM A lazy, seemingly unmotivated puppy who makes taking a walk a real chore. *See* COUCH POTATO.

BUMPER Short-nosed dogs tend to look as if they "bumped" into walls. Good name for a Bulldog, Boston Terrier, Boxer, Bullmastiff or Pug.

BUMPKIN Born and bred for the country life.

BUNK It is all bunk that a puppy needs a big house and yard to be happy. Try some training and a lot of love instead.

BUNNY No garden is safe from this digging, munching puppy.

BURGER A puppy with this name has probably ruined one barbecue too many.

BURLY A powerhouse puppy who shows off by carrying objects heavier than his own weight. Barbells might be a favorite toy of this one.

BURP She'd say, "Excuse me," if she could speak.

BUSTER Common name for an uncommon dog.

BUTTER Sweet and creamy. You will want to make this one an ingredient in all you do. Good name for a buff Cocker Spaniel, yellow Labrador, Golden Retriever or Soft Coated Wheaten Terrier.

BUTTERBALL Puppies who tend to stuff themselves occasionally need to be reminded that what is cute and chubby to you might be dinner to someone else.

BUTTERCUP *See* BUTTER.

BUTTERMILK *See* BUTTER.

BUTTERSCOTCH Sure to bring some sweetness into your life.

BUTTS Be careful. Puppies love the smell of tobacco and this pup might just develop some bad habits if you don't keep a close eye on him.

BUZZ This pest of a puppy looks and acts like a bug. *See* BUG.

BUZZARD This one probably earned his or her name by swooping down on anything within reach. Countless shoes, pillows, panty hose and socks have already fallen prey.

C.C. Short for Chow Chow or Chinese Crested.

CABARET This one-dog show will turn your life into a cabaret, old chum.

CABOODLE A puppy with this name is probably the final addition to your menagerie, or so you claim.

CABOOSE The smallest of the litter.

CADBURY *See* CHOCOLATE.

CADET The youngest, newest member of the family.

CADILLAC Big Daddy always gets his way.

CAIRO Named after this Egyptian city, your traveling puppy will go to the ends of the world with you.

CAJUN Your pup, much like these people, might have a palate for spicy foods.

CALAMITY The disaster subsides after puppyhood.

CALIBER Good for a potentially fine show dog of any breed, with the brains to match.

CALIFORNIA This puppy has a laid-back attitude and style all his or her own.

CAMEMBERT *See* Brie *in Chapter 1.*

CAMEO After just one performance from this shy puppy you knew you had to have her.

CANDY Just doesn't get any sweeter than this puppy.

CAPER Is there anything missing around the house since this puppy arrived?

CAPTAIN This brash young sea dog has a hard time taking commands.

CARAMBA Aaaay Caramba! The damage a puppy can do.

CARAMEL This silky brown pup will satisfy anyone's sweet tooth. Good for an Irish Setter.

CARAMELO A mixture of Chocolate and Caramel. Good name for a dark, brindle dog.

CARGO You had to smuggle this puppy home.

CARNATION Special occasions are not the only time you will want to show off this stylish puppy.

CAROB The healthy alternative to any life-style.

CASANOVA It's okay to give your heart to this little lover, if he doesn't steal it first.

CASH This one cost you plenty of cold hard . . . , but was worth every penny of it.

CASTAWAY Lost and forgotten, this one didn't have a collar, let alone a bed, before you picked him up.

CATAMARAN With the wind at his back this puppy seemingly sails through life.

CAYENNE See Jalapeño.

CEREBRUM An advanced puppy who, with this name, should be given the opportunity to partake in all the schooling available. You better hope he passes basic obedience. Comical name for a seemingly "slow" puppy.

CHA-CHA This adorable little one will dance her way right into your heart.

CHABLIS This puppy will only get better with time.

CHALET Typical of the Swiss Alps, like the Bernese and Greater Swiss Mountain dogs, this dwelling place is one of enormous charm—just like your wonderful, new puppy.

CHALLENGER There is no task too difficult or lesson too hard for this puppy when he or she knows that a treat is the ultimate reward.

CHAMPAGNE Time to celebrate. This puppy is the best present you could ever hope for.

CHAMPION Good nickname is "Champ," but he doesn't need a title to earn this name; stellar performances around the house will be enough.

CHANEL A chic, worldly puppy.

CHANTILLY Be sure to dress this precious pup in lace.

CHAOS is this pup's first, middle and last name.

CHARADE This puppy leaves good clues as to what makes him or her happy.

CHARMER You will have a hard time keeping the girls away from this less-than-bashful pup.

CHAUFFEUR This protective pooch loves nothing more than going everywhere with you.

CHECK For a puppy who really knows how to corner you.

CHECKERS Jumping is one of his or her favorite hobbies.

CHEDDAR Good for a snack-loving pup that smiles when you say "cheese."

CHEERLEADER This puppy's enthusiasm never ceases to amaze you.

CHEETAH Learn to run in the opposite direction with lots of toys and treats in hand in order to catch this fast puppy, because trying to beat him on foot is nearly impossible.

CHEW-CHEW Getting this stubborn little puppy to relinquish her chew toys may become a source of amusement for the family. Hence, this name is good for a puppy who gets very attached to toys.

CHEWY *See* CHEW-CHEW.

CHIC Fashionable and well-groomed is how you'll have to keep this style-setter. May we suggest you locate the poshest doggie boutiques in town?

CHICLET Sometimes the smallest bits pack the most power.

CHICORY A puppy with a dark brown coat is appropriate for this name.

CHIEF Crazy puppy antics will in time be interpreted as wise decisions, hopefully. This name was worn by the first Saint Bernard registered with the AKC, in 1885.

CHIFFON Silky, smooth and sexy, like the beautiful coat of your new pet.

CHILI This pup knows how to warm you on a cold day.

CHIN-CHIN Good name for a Chinese Shar-Pei because this breed, like this health food craze, is both trendy and Chinese.

CHINA As beautiful and precious as a china doll, this pup should be dainty, refined and have eyes of innocence. Also a good comical name for breeds possessing other than delicate qualities.

CHINA DOLL *See* CHINA.

CHIP A real chip off the old block. This guy will worship the ground you walk on, so be careful. Puppies learn from their owners. He might pick up some of your bad habits. No chewing your nails, between-meal snacking or playing in the mud.

CHIPMUNK A puppy with this name might eat so much that it seems he or she is storing up for winter.

CHIPPER You can't get much happier than this pup. In fact, his or her early morning enthusiasm might be a bit much to handle.

CHIPS *See* CHIP.

CHIQUITA Good name for a female yellow Labrador.

CHIVAS A regal Skye Terrier, Scottish Deerhound or Gordon Setter would wear this title with royal ease.

CHOCOLATA *See* CHOCOLATE.

CHOCOLATE Good name for a chocolate Labrador, or any dog displaying smooth, rich chocolate coloring. Hopefully your dog did not earn this name due to his or her eating habits.

CHOO-CHOO This little engine of a puppy could.

CHOPPER His or her twirling, flying and landing abilities will never cease to amaze you.

CHOPSTICKS Good for any pup whose skinny legs move as though coordination appears impossible.

CHOWDER A gluttonous puppy.

CHUBBY Most puppies grow out of their puppy fat, so try not to make this one live up to his or her cuddly name.

CHUBFISH This water-loving puppy looks like he or she will sink before learning to swim—but don't bet on it.

CHUMP A pushy pup.

CHUNK Resembling the Hulk, a dog with this name should be low to the ground and packed with muscle. His or her body is more square than rectangular.

CHUNKY *See* CHUBBY.

CINDER In the movie *101 Dalmatians* the Dalmatian pups covered themselves with cinders to protect their beautiful coats from being made into human garments. This name is good for a rescued Dalmatian or any dog having a smoky-colored coat; some Italian Greyhounds, Neapolitan Mastiffs and Weimaraners.

CINNAMON BEAR Sweet and cuddly, like any and all puppies.

CITRUS *See O.J. in Chapter 3.*

CLASSY Only the finest meats delivered by the butcher himself will do for this puppy.

CLICHÉ Ordinary-looking at first glance, but his or her personality is unique. Good name for any dog that is more individual than you might think.

CLIPPER Like a fast sailing ship, a puppy with this name can cut through a dense furniture-filled room rather swiftly.

CLONE Next thing you know she or he will want to eat what you do and sleep where you do, or has that already happened?

CLOVER This puppy might just be your lucky charm.

COCONUT At times it would appear that this puppy's head is filled with coconut milk instead of brains.

COCOPUFF Good name for a little brown furball of a Pekingese, Pomeranian or chocolate-colored Poodle puppy.

COGNAC Like a fine cordial, you could not be in better company than with this puppy when winding down your day.

COMET Fast as a streaking comet and with a magical twinkle in his or her eyes, this is a rare and beautiful pup.

CONDOR Like California Condors, well-trained puppies seem, at times, destined for extinction. Maybe your sharp puppy can help reverse the trend.

CONFETTI Little "pieces" of puppyhood are probably strewn all over your house. You will be finding remnants for years to come.

CONJURER You never know what this puppy might be cooking up next. THis was the name of the first Curly-Coated Retriever registered with the AKC, in 1924.

COOKIE This fiendish pup with an extreme sweet tooth has been caught one too many times with his or her paw in the cookie jar.

COON A creature of the night. Good name for Coonhounds or any dog whose face markings suggest a mask.

COOTER Resembling an old coot, this puppy looks old before his or her time, like a Chinese Shar-Pei.

COPPER See a penny, pick it up, . . . and he or she will forever bring you good luck. Good name for a rescue puppy.

COQUETTE Flirtatious and at times demure, this baby knows how to get what she wants.

CORAL The animal that adds so much beauty to the undersea world has now moved above sea level and into your home. Congratulations.

CORDIAL Gracious and soothing, this one has all the nice qualities of a nightcap.

CORI Less formal version of CORAL.

CORKY An old favorite. This has proven itself to never wear thin.

CORONET For a puppy who likes to toot his own horn.

COSMO(POLITAN) *Très* chic.

COTTON White, fluffy and a 100 percent Bichon Frise, Maltese or white Poodle.

COUCH POTATO (TATTI) More toys and exercise can never hurt.

COUNT This noble pup should be held in high esteem.

COURVOISIER She or he warms your heart and lifts your spirits.

COWBOY Obedience school will probably be a chore. This puppy may have more luck taming you. But don't give up!

COWGIRL This one will have more luck sweet-talking you out of obedience school than attending.

CRACKER A slang term for a lover of the beach and relaxed living, like most puppies and coastal dwellers.

CRANBERRY A round, sweet, little puppy.

CRASH You might want to find a helmet or good insurance policy for this reckless pup.

CRESCENT For the confused puppy, who bays at the moon even when it isn't full.

CRICKET The noises this one makes can keep you up all night, especially if she's sharing your pillow or if she escaped from her sleeping quarters.

CRIER Nothing seems to pacify this puppy, or maybe you just haven't figured out the joys of puppyhood yet. More toys never hurt.

CRIMSON This puppy's antics in public are sure to make you blush.

CRISTYL A colorful, reflective puppy whose love seems to possess healing qualities.

CRITTER It's hard to tell what comprises this pup. A few mammalian qualities, a few reptilian, and maybe even some aquatic. You not only aren't sure where he or she came from, but also what is going to grow next: fur, scales, even flippers are possible on your lovable beast.

CROISSANT Good for your little Papillon or French Bulldog.

CROUTON A puppy with this name is usually found nearby when mealtime rolls around. Good name for a Toy dog.

CRUISER Better give this one a curfew and make sure he's wearing his tags. He likes to stay out late and often gets into a tad of trouble. Keep the number of your local humane shelter taped to the refrigerator at all times. Better still, let him be a "Cruiser" in name only!

CRUMB No need to buy a vacuum cleaner. You have your puppy instead.

CRUMPET English tea and crumpets might be one of her favorite treats. Good name for a Toy Manchester Terrier or a Yorkie.

CRUNCHER Appropriate name for a puppy purchased before or during his or her teething stage. Whether it be chew toys or chair legs this puppy manages to crunch through just about anything.

CRUSADER If there's a cause, he's found it: too many bones in the garbage, damsel in distress, kitten up a tree?

CRYBABY Whimpering and whining are this puppy's forte.

CUBBY Good for a pup who resembles a bear cub. *See* BEAR.

CUCKOO Does your puppy chase shadows, stare at walls, become obsessed with meaningless little toys and run in aimless circles? If he doesn't, he might be crazy.

CUDDLES Good name for a dog who thinks he or she is a lap dog, no matter how large.

CUPCAKE For a puppy as sweet as her name.

CUTIE *See* CUTIE PIE.

CUTIE PIE So adorable you just won't be able to keep your hands off her.

DAKOTA A dog with this name will love the great outdoors.

DALLAS This one is a living testament that everything in Dallas is big. Good name for a Great Dane or Mastiff.

DAMAGE A pup with a name like this should come accompanied with care or disarming instructions. Comical name for a docile puppy.

DAMSEL One who often seems in distress.

DANCER This pup makes chasing his or her tail look graceful.

DANDELION For a puppy who is already growing faster than you thought possible.

DAREDEVIL An honors student in doggie agility class. You should take out extensive insurance coverage on this daring puppy.

DASH This puppy will put just a dash of spice into your life. It was the name of the first Dachshund registered with the AKC, in 1885.

DAWN This pup is usually up before you and seems to relish early morning hours, much to your chagrin.

DAZZLER Good name for an Afghan Hound, a royal dog descended from the exotic East. Can't you just picture this dog poised next to your armchair? She could make you feel like royalty.

DÉJÀ VU Didn't you just clean up that mess?

DEBUTANTE A highly social pup who loves having company.

COUCH POTATO

WANTED!!

HEIGHT : 6 INCHES
WEIGHT : 5 POUNDS
EYES : BROWN

WANTED FOR SHOE STEALING AND ALL 'ROUND
HOUSEHOLD ANNHILATION CALL 1-800-DOG-
GONE

DESPERADO

DEEOGEE D.O.G.

DERBY Good name for dogs destined to grow to horse size.

DESPERADO A loner pup who attempts to climb fences.

DETONATOR An explosive personality makes this pup all the more lovable.

DETOUR A stubborn, relentless demeanor makes this pup a daily, yet welcomed deviation in your normal routine.

DEVIL Good name for a playfully mischievous puppy, but be careful, puppies sometimes grow into their names.

DEW Like soft morning dew, this pup will dampen your cheeks with kisses during the early morning hours if you don't rise and shine when he or she wishes.

DEXEDRINE Having more energy than imaginable.

DIAMOND in the rough. You found yours.

DICE Good name for a Dalmatian.

DIDDLEY This one likes to diddle the day away, whether it be by napping, romping or hanging out by the refrigerator.

DIGBY Sounds good. If you come up with an anecdote for this name, let us know.

DIGGER Destroyer of gardens, mud-stainer of carpets and all-round true piglet.

DINO Looking a bit prehistoric. Appropriate name for a Dogue de Bordeaux or Neapolitan Mastiff.

DIXIE You better whistle the right tune if you want this pup to come running back.

DIZZY If the name fits—wear it.

DOC Your love and affection is what this puppy prescribes.

DOGLET Much like a pig in behavior, but having paws instead of hooves, which can lead only to the conclusion that you have purchased a cross between a puppy and a piglet.

DOMINO This one has the uncanny ability to create a chain reaction, whether it be through love or troublemaking. Appropriate for a Dalmatian or Harlequin Great Dane. Comical for a solid-colored dog.

DON *See* HONCHO.

DOODLE A puppy with this name will tend to leave his or her mark everywhere. The carpet and drapes are his or her easel, so don't buy new ones until puppyhood is over ... in about fifteen years.

DOTS Good name for a Dalmatian, or for your carpet after housebreaking.

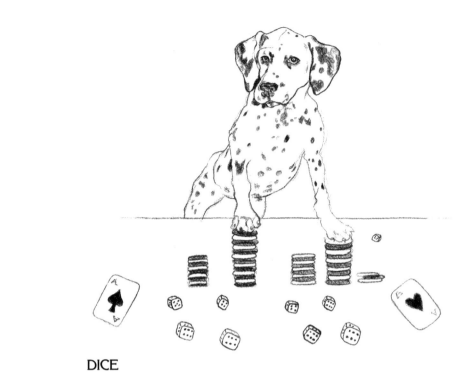

DICE

DOZER

DOUGH-BOY This pudgy pup squeals with delight when you hug him.

DOZER As in "bull." Able to move backyards, kennels and helpless kittens in a single bound.

DRAGON A steadfast protector of your home.

DREAMER For a puppy who will thoroughly enjoy napping his or her days away.

DREAMWEAVER Her company can get you through the night.

DRUMMER This pup pounds out a tune anytime, day or night, but no need to worry, maybe he'll grow into his talent.

DUCHESS A little royalty dresses up any home. *See* PRINCESS.

DUDE A cool pup who likes to wear his baseball cap backwards. Good for a Bull Terrier or any other dog with the attitude that fits.

DUDETTE The Number One lady friend of a dude, especially if the dude is her adoring owner.

DUFFY A long-standing favorite. Especially good for any male dog of an Irish or Scottish breed; Westie fans love it!

DUMPLING This little piglet enjoys stuffing herself until she's near explosion. Be careful how much and what you feed her, and definitely omit pork from her diet. We wouldn't want her mistaken for a pot sticker. Good name for a Basset Hound.

DUNK Bobbing for apples may be an interesting game for this water-loving puppy.

DUSTMOP This little ball of fur will be able to earn his or her keep with cleaning talents, and can probably double as a vacuum, ensuring spotless floors. Good name for a Lhasa Apso, Maltese, Shih Tzu or Yorkshire Terrier and a reminder not to fall behind on the grooming.

DUSTY This one, reminiscent of Linus in the Charles Schulz comic strip "Peanuts," kicks up dust wherever he or she goes.

DWEEB You won't be able to resist this misfit.

DYNAMITE *See* DETONATOR.

DYNAMO This pup's energy will never cease to amaze you.

ECHO It might take at least twice before your pup learns this name.

ECLIPSE For the puppy who insists on walking in front of the television set when you are trying to watch it.

EDGE To say this puppy pushes your patience to the edge is putting it mildly. A few more walks will calm you both.

DUSTMOP

EGGO A puppy with this name simply won't let go. Tug-of-war is her favorite game.

ELF A happy-go-lucky companion who all but whistles while he or she works.

EMERALD Walk this jewel of a pup down the street and everyone will be green with envy.

ENCHILADA You got the whole enchilada and nothing less when you brought this puppy home.

ENERGIZER A high-strung puppy who is never short on energy.

EPIC Larger than life. This small pup makes a great and timeless impression.

EQUITY This one might have cost you a pretty penny, but he or she is definitely a worthwhile and long-term investment.

ESCAPADE A conventional puppy full of unconventional maneuvers.

ESCORT A faithful companion who will always be at your side.

ESKIMO Cold nose, warm heart. Good for an Alaskan Malamute.

EXCALIBUR A stubborn stick-in-the-mud of a puppy who likes things his or her way. Motivating this puppy might resemble pulling a sword from a stone.

FACE Just look at that face. It's hard to keep your hands off, but no cheek pinching please.

FANCY Good name for a well-groomed Miniature Poodle or Bichon Frise.

FANDANGO This puppy will always be two steps ahead of you.

FANG See Nosferatu *in Chapter 1.*

FATAL BEAUTY Exercise caution when giving your heart to this one, she might just turn out to be the love of your life.

FATSO *See* Fatty.

FATTY Fatty, two-by-four, can't get through the doggie door. Better cut back on the treats.

FENDER (BENDER) An accident-prone pup who should be watched carefully and fully insured.

FIDO You can't beat it for a classic!

FIFI Oh, please! Even a Poodle couldn't hold its head up with this name—or could it? You decide.

FIGARO Good name for a "vocal" puppy.

FINK Notorious for making other puppies look bad, this beautiful puppy will always slip away clean.

FIREBUG This puppy has a fascination with fireflies. At night he or she will be seen busily running about the yard after them.

FIRECRACKER This puppy is prone to extreme bursts of activity.

FISHBONE Often a pacifier for cats, this fishbone fails to put them at ease.

FIZZ A spirited, lively pup.

FLANNEL Soft, warm and traditional, this puppy will get cozier with age.

FLAPPER Yes sir, that's my baby, no sir, don't mean maybe. Yes sir, *you're* my baby now. Good name for a Boston Terrier. *See* OPAL *in Chapter 1.*

FLASH Breaking all sound barriers the instant food hits his or her bowl.

FLICKER This twinkling little pup shines brighter than the rest.

FLING Far from a one-night stand, this puppy deserves and yearns for a long-term relationship.

FLIRT This puppy will make a lot of friends at the park.

FLOWER This beautiful blossom might just wilt all the others in the garden.

FLUFFY Comical name for a short-haired dog.

FLURRY All puppies deserve a constant flurry of attention.

FLUSH This royal flush beats about any other one around. Also the name of Elizabeth Barrett Browning's Cocker Spaniel companion.

FLY GIRL This puppy's got the latest moves.

FOOTBALL Always the center of attention, especially on Sunday afternoons.

FOXY An attractive female puppy.

FRECKLES Tailor-made for a Dalmatian, but it also suited Richard Nixon's famous Cocker.

FREEBIE This puppy's love comes free of charge.

FREEWAY Between trips to the vet, visits to the park and pet store, obedience school and housebreaking routine, this puppy is acquainting you with the fast lane.

FRISBEE An acrobatic natural, bound to be the center of attention at the park. This puppy is probably named after his or her favorite toy.

FRISKY This name might give your puppy a cat complex. Only use it if you don't mind him or her being very independent and forever scaling neighborhood trees.

FROGGY Passing the days aimlessly chasing flies with his or her oversized tongue will be routine for this fur-covered amphibian wannabe.

FU MAN CHU The name of a fictitious Chinese villain who was described as having a moustache similar to those worn by Shih Tzus.

FU MING CHU Female counterpart to Fu Man Chu.

FUDDLES The simplest of tasks might be difficult for this lovably fumbling puppy.

FUDGE The color of this puppy is unmistakable. *See* CHOCOLATE.

FUNGUS This wrinkled little puppy would rather be out playing in the mud than doing just about anything else.

FUNKY Your puppy is noticeably in step with today.

FUNNYGIRL *See* BABS *in Chapter 3.*

FURBALL There must be a dog in there somewhere.

FURFACE Eyes? Check. Nose? Check. Hanging tongue? Check. Good name for a Komondor, Old English Sheepdog, Puli, Shih Tzu or other very furry friend.

FURR For a puppy who has more hair than he or she knows what to do with.

FUNGUS

GATOR

FUZZIE Wuzzie was a bear. Fuzzie Wuzzie had no hair. Cute name for a Xoloitzcuintli or maybe a Hairless Chinese Crested.

GAMBLER This risk-taking puppy might make both you and your veterinarian nervous with his or her crazy antics.

GARLIC A puppy with this name will be manageable only in small doses.

GATEKEEPER A born guard pup. Nobody will get through your door without this puppy's security clearance.

GATOR If cats start missing from the neighborhood an X ray of this clown may be in order.

GEEKIE *See* DWEEB.

GEEZER Appropriate for young puppies who look old, whether due to their expressions or physical traits: Bulldogs, Chinese Shar-Peis and Pugs are good candidates.

GENIUS Jonathan Swift once wrote, "When a true genius appears in the world you may know him by this sign, that the dunces are all in confederacy against him." Remember this when everybody is mad at the poor puppy for getting into the garbage. Who left the garbage where the puppy could reach it?

GERBIL Resembling a rodent more than a dog, this name is good for a puppy from one of the Toy breeds.

GHIRADELLI *See* CHOCOLATE.

GHOSTBUSTER For the puppy who barks at and chases empty space.

GIDDY A lighthearted pooch who will find humor and amusement in most everything.

GIGGLES Good name for the dog who seems to be laughing at you when you expect him or her to obey your commands.

GIGOLO Love and affection come cheap and in abundance from this pup.

GINGER A sexy little puppy the color of ginger: light brown.

GINGERSNAP A variation on GINGER and a good name for any sweet, small dog of the right color.

GIPPER Win one for the old what?

GIRL Sugar and spice and everything nice comprise this little puppy.

GIRLFRIEND There's no telling what this puppy will do if you fail to keep her happy. May we suggest occasional presents for no real reason?

GLADSTONE This happy puppy will love nothing more than spending afternoons skipping stones at the beach.

GOBBLE Gobble, gobble, is the way this puppy inhales every morsel you give him or her.

GOBLIN Don't be fooled by this little ghoul. Under his or her costume is a true angel.

GOOBER As messy and gooey as this pup will get, he's worth it.

GOOCH A cross between a pooch and a gorilla, this hybrid puppy has all the physical characteristics of a dog while still thinking he can climb on your furniture and eat off the fine china.

GOOMBA This puppy is the head of the family.

GOOSE A puppy with this name probably has a pure white coat that is soft as feathers. He or she will keep you warm on cold nights if you allow on-the-bed snuggling.

GOPHER This ground-dwelling rodent loves to burrow through your garden. Hopefully your puppy will not follow suit!

GORGEOUS With drool hanging from your puppy's tongue and mud-stained paws, who could argue with this name?

GORILLA Like the great ape—burly-looking but a sensitive soul.

GOUDA This puppy's aroma might be mildly reminiscent.

GRANDEUR A puppy's love is larger than life.

GREMLIN No one really knows what planet creatures that look like your puppy come from, but we are fairly sure it isn't Earth. Be careful not to expose him or her to too much water or sunlight. You never know what could happen.

Good name for a Boston Terrier, French Bulldog, Brussels Griffon or Pug.

GRITS This Southern belle (or beau) of a puppy is an important part of your every morning.

GRIZZLY *See* BEAR.

GRUMPUS This pup appears to always be getting up on the wrong side of the doggie bed.

GRUMPY Bouts of depression and an attitude are traits found in this puppy who will make demands and sulk more than he or she should. With antics like this he or she will probably have you well trained.

GRUNGE Not the tidiest of puppies, but possibly the cutest.

GRUNION Good name for a dog who loves to flap aimlessly around on the beach when the tide comes in.

GRUNT Good name for a puppy who seems to possess piglike qualities. Are you sure you saw his or her parents?

GUCCI There is enough prestige in this puppy's pedigree to compensate for his or her earthy mischievousness.

GUFFAW An accident-prone puppy will earn this name.

GUIDO This "wiseguy" puppy has a tough air about him.

GUMBALL In the corner, under the bed, between the sheets, you just never know where this round little puppy will come up next.

GUMDROP An old-fashioned favorite.

GUMMIE BEAR Sweet and clinging.

GUNG HO Calmness will hopefully come with age for this anxious little pup.

GUNNER A puppy with this name must have an explosive personality.

GUSTO For a puppy who fills with enthusiasm when he or she hears any of the following: ride, park, walk, food, toy—quite an extensive vocabulary for a little puppy.

GYRO Contortionism is apparently one of this puppy's hobbies, making him or her an accomplished escape artist.

HACKI-SACK Maybe there are beans in his or her head with the way this puppy bounces around.

HALCYON A calming puppy who will make the toughest times a little easier.

HALEY Fast as a streaking comet. This speeding bullet will mesmerize most who catch a glimpse.

HAM Here is a puppy not afraid of looking silly in public.

HANDSOME Looks can get him everywhere ... the sofa, the bed, the car, maybe even the dinner table.

HANNIBAL (the Cannibal) Sly. Will do anything for a cut of meat.

HAPPY Don't you just love a puppy with no complaints?

HAPPY FEET A proud little trotter.

HARD ROCK The photos and memorabilia of this classic puppy may be valuable someday, at least to you.

HARDY He will brave any storm for his beloved owners.

HARLEY A very *cooooool* puppy who loves to ride.

HARMONY You can skip puppy socialization classes, this baby already gets along with everybody.

HAVOC The name says it all. Training should be started early.

HAWK Having the keenest senses around, this puppy can hear an intruder, or the opening of the refrigerator door, from a mile away.

HAZER This puppy will pledge his loyalty to you.

HEARTBREAKER A puppy with this name will be seemingly indifferent to the flood of attention she or he receives.

HEARTS *See* HEARTBREAKER.

HEDGEHOG A ground-dwelling, mud-slinging, grunter of a pup.

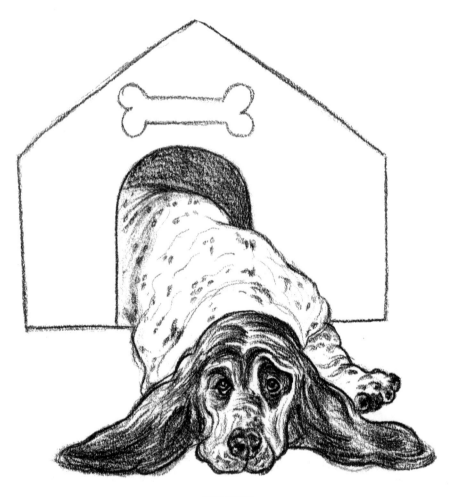

HERMIT

HEFTY Definitely not a wimpy pup.

HEIRESS The real princess of the house. Second in line for the cedar bed.

HERMIT For the pup who uncharacteristically doesn't like to go out much. He or she would rather just be home with you.

HERO Give him time.

HERSHEY Good name for a chocolate Labrador or a brown Poodle.

HICKORY Reminiscent of the open prairies. This name well suits any dog from one of the herding breeds.

HIPPO Easygoing water-dwelling mammals remind you of your puppy who naps the days away.

HISTORIA For the academic's dog.

HOBO Lost and abandoned without even a hobo sack of bones, now he or she has a softer life, thanks to you.

HOG You let him sleep in bed, but you never discussed sharing the covers.

HOLLYWOOD For a showoff puppy who likes center stage.

HOMEBOY This territorial puppy is happiest on his home turf.

HONCHO Even at an early age this one will try to show you who's boss.

HONEY The sweetest puppy of them all. Good for like-colored dogs.

HONEY BEAR Always a sweet delight.

HONEYBEE *See* HONEY.

HONKY-TONK For the puppy that always gets a smile from you—like listening to ragtime rhythm.

HOOD This mischievous little puppy might get you into trouble with the neighbors if left unattended at night.

HOOFMAN Resembling a horse, or maybe a cow, this puppy's big paws are already capable of trampling anything in his path.

HOOLIGAN *See* HOOD.

HOPE Man's best friend.

HOT DOG Good name for a Dachshund, or any hot little pup.

HOTSHOT This name might boost your puppy's ego to intolerable levels, but maybe his or hers is already there.

HOWLER You can expect some long nights with a puppy bearing this name.

HUBBA HUBBA For an adorable, sexy female puppy who the boys won't be able to keep their eyes off.

HUMDINGER This puppy is both physically and characteristically striking.

HUNTER Do neighborhood cats seem to be disappearing? Good name for a hunting aficionado's dog.

HUNTRESS Feminine counterpart of HUNTER.

HURRICANE Destruction may be left in this pup's path if not trained properly.

ICE-T Good for a Rottweiler.

ICEMAN Appropriate name for a puppy who enjoys the great, cold outdoors: Great Pyrenees, Newfoundlands, Saint Bernards, all the sled dog breeds and a host of others easily qualify.

IGGY This nickname for "iguana" suggests the traits of this lovable reptile: easy adaptability, good house pet, friendly, rare and lazy. Does your puppy qualify?

IGLOO Good name for an Alaskan Malamute, Siberian Husky, Samoyed or any other breed well suited for cold winters.

INDIA Unique and exotic in her own right.

INDIAN This puppy is a red-blooded American, like the Boston Terrier.

INDIANA Vast cornfields, rock quarries and open, snow-covered fields make good playgrounds for this Midwestern puppy. *See* HOOSIER *in Chapter 1.*

INFINITY This puppy will love you till the end of time.

INKY A Rorschach test could be given on this puppy's patched markings.

INTELECTUS A snobbishly smart dog should be given this name, just as his or her predecessor was: Doberman Intelectus, the first Doberman Pinscher registered with the AKC, in 1908.

IODINE This puppy may take a little getting used to at first, but he or she will be very therapeutic in the long run. *See* RED.

IRRESISTIBLE It will be hard to keep your hands off this pup.

IVY This pup just won't stop growing!

J.B. A rare pup with a long, distinguished heritage.

JACKPOT A real winner!

JADE Your Chow Chow or Pekingese puppy, like this beautiful mineral, is a treasure of the Orient.

JAILBAIT A very young, alluring flirt of a puppy.

JALAPEÑO For a pupy whose antics will add a bit of a kick to your life.

JAMAICA A laid-back puppy—like life in the islands.

JAZZ Rhythm is in his blood. Just watch that tail go.

JELLY BEAN Every flavor is yummy to this sweet-toothed puppy.

JELLY-BELLY For a puppy who sort of jiggles while she walks.

JERSEY A rough-looking puppy with a bit of an attitude.

JET Black is the color of this puppy's coat.

JIGSAW Trying to put together this puppy's heritage will definitely be puzzling.

JINGLES The cat of the house will appreciate a few bells on this puppy's collar.

JINX Maybe you have just found the potion to break a spell of bad luck . . . an adorable puppy and lots of love.

JITTERBUG You have a real dancing machine on your hands.

JOKER This puppy is quite a wild card. You never know when or where he is going to pop up.

JOY is what this beautiful dog will bring to you.

JUBILEE Celebration is always in order when a new baby comes home.

JUDGE A puppy with this name will make the rules in the house.

JULEP No need to hide your medicine in drinks anymore. This puppy's love should cure all your ailments.

JUMBO Size isn't everything. Cute name for a tiny puppy with a huge personality.

JUNE Summertime is funtime for this wonderful June baby.

JUNIOR A real member of the family.

JUSTUS An understanding puppy.

K.O. This pooch is a knockout. *See* BOMBSHELL.

KATMANDU If this puppy ever runs away you know where he or she is goin'.

KEEPERS At first glance you knew this puppy was for keeps.

KELLOGG Breakfast might be your puppy's favorite meal, but dry kibble instead of cereal will be healthier for him or her.

KENO You hit the jackpot with this puppy.

KENYA *See* NAIROBI.

KEWPIE Having a round, cherubic face, this one should be dressed with red bows in her hair at all times.

KIBBLES Desperately seeking Bits.

KID You have mistaken your puppy for either a goat or a human, probably the latter.

KIKI A name such as this is sweet and rolls off the tongue easily, which will deter you from resorting to nicknames when using baby talk.

KILLER Good name for a small, sweet-looking dog.

KILO An exaggerated descriptive name for an adorably paunchy puppy.

KING No matter how many dogs have worn this name, there is no other like your puppy.

KINKO A few quirks add character.

KISSES See Baci *in Chapter 1.*

KLONDIKE See Yukon *in Chapter 1.*

KNICKERBOCKER This New York puppy might need to dress warmly in the winter. Good name for small, purse-size dogs whose owners dress them in sweaters.

KNOCKOUT A male pup who will probably earn a reputation for being feisty, or an attractive female pup.

KNUCKLES For a puppy with large, bony paws. *See* Paws.

KODA This name sounds like one that belongs to a strong, African tribal leader. Maybe it suits your Rhodesian Ridgeback puppy as well.

KOOL All the other dogs in the neighborhood will aspire to emulate this laid-back, suave puppy.

KORBEL Champagne is suitable for the celebratory occasion of bringing a new puppy home, especially one with this festive name.

KOSMIC Bound for universal greatness. Maybe you have another Lassie on your hands.

KRISPY A puppy with this name probably enjoys crunching his or her kibble very loudly. *See* BACON.

KRYPTONITE This puppy can find the weak spot in any Superman.

LABYRINTH Your house will become a maze of puppy toys for this beautifully spoiled puppy.

LAMBCHOP Your puppy is a luscious morsel, but you'd never eat her!

LAMBORGHINI A fast, powerful and loud puppy.

LASER It may be hard to see this puppy coming. And he will definitely have an impact on your life.

LASHES Good name for a yellow Labrador or Golden Retriever whose sweet lashes accent his or her beautiful eyes.

LAVENDER *See* LILAC *in Chapter 1.*

LEMON A puppy who appears to be the "lemon" of the litter will inevitably turn out to be the most spoiled.

LEVI An American classic, just like a Boston Terrier, Cocker Spaniel or Chesapeake Bay Retriever.

LIABILITY It's too bad you can't write off the damages and expenses incurred by puppyhood, but she will be worth every penny of it.

LIBERTY This stubborn puppy will forever insist on doing as she pleases.

LICKUMS For the puppy who loves to give kisses.

LIGHTNING Will always follow the damage caused by THUNDER.

LIGHTNING BUG *See* FIREBUG.

LINK to your heart.

LION Good name for a Little Lion Dog, or any puppy whose demands are occasionally voiced in the sound of a roar.

LIPS You will never have to beg for a kiss from this affectionate puppy.

LITMUS Things might change colors in your house or wardrobe due to this puppy's presence.

LITTLE GUY The smallest fella in the family.

LITTLE ONE This nickname for the baby of the family works just as well for your puppy's real name.

LIZARD Thin, fast and slippery, like a high-strung puppy.

LOONY Maybe there really is a screw loose somewhere. Have you seen a doctor recently?

LOVE-BUG All puppies are love-bugs at heart.

LOVE-PIG A combination of a LOVER and a PIGGY. *See Chapter 1 for* PIGGY *and below for* LOVER.

LOVER This puppy will forever steal the pillow and blankets.

LOVERBOY He will readily give and receive affection.

LOVERGIRL One bat of her eyelashes is all it takes to melt your heart.

LOVESONG This puppy's tune will melt your heart more than any of your old favorites.

LOVEY DOVEY *See* LOVER.

LULLABY Anything to get this puppy to sleep: cedar beds, teddy bears, down pillows, chew-chews, even a lullaby.

LUNATIC It will just take a little time before this puppy calms down. In the meantime, practicing his or her obedience commands can't hurt.

MAC-ATTACK This puppy's cravings will sometimes overpower his or her obedience training.

MACHO Good name for a small, docile dog.

MACINTOSH This puppy will be the apple of your eye.

MAESTRO For the puppy who will dictate and conduct your life.

MAFIOSO A puppy with this name will usually get what he wants.

MAGIC This puppy's antics will definitely defy imagination.

MAGNET You will have a magnetic attraction to this puppy.

MAHOGANY Well suited for an attractive dog of this color.

MAILMAN Hopefully this puppy will not earn his or her name.

MAJOR He hit the big leagues when he found you.

MANNERS will improve after puppyhood.

MAPLE SYRUP Thick and sappy. Good name for a dramatic pup who begs a lot.

MARAUDER Raiding and pillaging his toy chest will be a favorite pastime of this pup.

MARBLE "Sharp as a marble" may be the phrase used by your puppy's obedience trainer. Good name for a puppy with piebald markings.

MARDI GRAS Put a few beads on this puppy's collar and you'll have a real social beast on your hands.

MARSHMALLOW *See* COTTON.

MAVERICK A personal trainer might be better than group obedience for this independent puppy who likes to do things his own way.

MAY flowers will brighten your household beyond belief.

McCOY This puppy is a real source of love and pride for you.

ME TOO A puppy with this name has already made it quite clear that he or she does not like to be left behind.

MEATLOAF Tuck those paws under his or her chubby belly and what does your puppy look like?

MELLOW Easygoing and easy to please.

MELODY This puppy's snoring will be music to your ears.

MELON-HEAD Not the smartest of puppies, but quite possibly the cutest.

MERCEDES This beautiful puppy will make you the envy of the neighborhood.

MESQUITE A puppy with this name will probably hover around the barbecue.

METRO You will be able to go just about anywhere with this puppy.

MIATA Trendy, small and fast; like the Jack Russell Terrier.

MIDGET Appropriate name for dogs who simply look like they should be larger: Miniature Pinschers, Miniature Schnauzers and Toy Poodles all fit the bill.

MIDNIGHT You never know what will happen when the clock strikes twelve, especially if your puppy has free run of the house at night. Appropriate name for black Labradors, Schipperkes or any other black dog.

MINK Good name for a puppy whose coat is soft, supple and inviting to touch.

MISERY This puppy will try to convince you that life without constant attention and treats is sheer misery. She may be right.

MISSING LINK Like the creature man has sought for centuries, this puppy probably appeared out of nowhere and looks as if he or she belongs to another age.

MOCHA This name suits any dog with a brownish-colored coat.

MOLE For the burrowing puppy who will only peek out of his or her blankets at the smell of food.

MONGOOSE Agile, small and feisty, like the Jack Russell Terrier.

MONKEY It seems this pup is related to humans somewhere along the evolutionary line, due to his or her apelike agility.

MOOCHY No amount of toys or treats will be enough to repay your puppy for all the love and affection you mooch off him or her, but a simple pat on the head will be a nice start.

MOODY This puppy will occasionally need to be humored and appeased, but his or her good moods are enough to uplift all around.

MOONBEAM or **MOONMIST** For the groovy puppy.

MOONDANCE Dancing in the moonlight may be one of this puppy's tricks, as long as you keep him on your own property.

MOONGODDESS This beautiful female puppy will turn into a literal goddess when the sun goes down, if you did not already know.

MOONRAKER A puppy with this name will be able to double as an astronaut, at least in his or her apparent ability to defy gravity.

MOONSTRUCK

MOONSTRUCK For a puppy who loves to bay at the moon.

MOOSE Good name for a Bloodhound.

MOPSY Resembling DustMOP. It will be hard to distinguish the facial features of this pup.

MOPTOP *See* DustMOP.

MOROCCO Your house will probably become a mecca of doggie toys and puppy obstacles.

MOUSTACHE Good name for dogs who will forever insist on dipping their furry moustache in their food and water bowls, such as any Schnauzer.

MOVADO With impeccable precision, this puppy will always know what time dinner is served.

MU SHU Good name for a special treat of a puppy that looks positively yummy.

MUDDLES The slightest alteration in routine can really muddle up this puppy's day.

MUDPIE Puddles will become the enemy.

MUENSTER A "sharp"-smelling puppy who at times acts a bit monstrous deserves this name.

MUFFIN Owners who love to talk baby talk to their puppy can get some mileage out of this name. But remember, if you don't use your puppy's real name often he or she will not learn it.

MUG *See* FACE.

MUNCHER For the puppy who insists on "munching" everything in sight.

MUNCHKIN Good name for a puppy who appears to be a small version of what he or she will look like as an adult.

MUNCHYKIN A miniature MUNCHKIN.

MUTANT Six toes, a pronounced underbite, bald spots . . . you get the picture.

MUTT An affectionate name for any puppy—regardless of background.

MYSTIC A little magic entered your home when this puppy arrived.

NAIROBI This puppy will frequently "safari" by him or herself around the neighborhood if the gate is left open.

NAVIGATOR Good companion for a parent who loves to hike.

NEON For a pup who will stand out wherever he or she goes.

NEWT A good name for a puppy that is as comfortable in the water as on dry ground.

NIBBLES It's doubtful that a puppy with this name is a picky eater. in fact, he or she probably nibbles on everything within reach.

NICKELS For a rescue puppy who barely cost more than a few nickels, but is worth a million.

NIFTY Maybe the fifties will come back.

NIGHTMARE Luckily this nightmare won't go away when you wake up.

NIKE Good name for a pooch who loves to run, hence, good name for just about any puppy.

NIPPER A puppy with this name will just love to join you for a nightly nip.

NISTKA A wildly imaginative puppy who is headed for success.

NITRO Active and inventive. Appropriate name for any very energetic dog.

NOISEMAKER The life of the party.

NOMAD Shifted from one home to the next, your new puppy will welcome your stability.

NUGGET Worth a fortune.

O.T.M. One too many? Never!

OL' SPORT A gentleman's dog.

OOGA-BOOGA This name has a good beat if you say it enough.

ORBIT Ears back and ready for takeoff. You never know where he or she will land.

OREO The good stuff is on the inside. Good for puppy with an all-black coat except for a white streak on his or her chest.

OUTRIGGER A must for any boat aficionado.

OUZO This puppy warms your heart and lifts your spirits.

OX Good name for a powerhouse of a puppy.

OZONE Layers and layers of puppyhood and affection are about to engulf your new, dog-filled life.

PADDY Cake, paddy cake, baker's man, bake this pup a cake . . . or suffer the consequences.

PAISLEY Good name for a piebald dog.

PAL Every person's best friend.

PANACHE This doggie will add a sense of style and flair to your life.

PANDA Like the giant panda, this omnivorous little puppy will feed on just about anything, if you don't keep a close eye on him or her.

PANDEMONIUM Much like your household since this pup with this name arrived.

PANSY Aggression is not in this one's demeanor.

PANTHER Svelte and quick.

PARADISE This puppy will not lead a rough life, thanks to you.

PARAGON A puppy with this name is bound to finish first in his or her obedience class.

PATCHES An old-time favorite name for a spotted puppy and a new original for a solid-colored dog.

PÂTÉ Probably derived as a joke, this name will invoke laughter, and maybe a little misguided fear, from anyone who hears it.

PATHFINDER This one will be a good hiking dog.

PATRIOT Loyalty and duty are inherent in this puppy.

PATSY Sounds like your cat named the new puppy.

PAUPER This puppy had nothing when you found him or her, and now you have nothing together.

PAWS For a young puppy who looks clumsy because his or her paws are growing faster than his or her body.

PEACHES Sometimes a little messy, but always wonderfully sweet, just like your new puppy.

PEANUTS Have you ever heard the expression, "He must have a brain the size of a peanut"? Well that was derived from a dog's reference to his owner when the owner expected the pooch to go outside in the rain.

PEEWEE A runt of a puppy.

PENN A writer's true companion.

PEPPER Good name for a Dalmatian. In a two-dog household a good name for the other dog is SALT.

PEPPERMINT A Christmas puppy, but refreshing all year round.

PEST *See* NUDGE *in Chapter 1.*

PEUGEOT Good name for a Basset Hound or Papillon.

PHANTOM Your shoes are missing. The carpet is stained. The cookies are gone, and the bed is a mess. There must be a ghost in the house.

PICKLES Good for a pup who adds a savory accent to your life.

PIGGLES-WIGGLES Children love this name.

PIGGY-WIGGY This puppy probably loves roast beef.

PING If brain damage has not already occurred, it's sure to set in if this puppy bounces off the walls anymore.

PINKY Like a baby finger or toe, this puppy is the littlest of the family.

PIPER Good name for a puppy who will undoubtedly be a leader.

PIRANHA Fingers and toes are sometimes mistaken for chewies by this puppy.

PIRATE Have shoes started missing since this kleptomaniac puppy moved in?

PISCES Good name for any water-loving puppy. Labradors and Poodles are good candidates.

PISTOL Fast and sharp. Make sure you know the responsibility involved before you bring this energetic puppy home.

PISTON A high-viscosity pup who already seems to burn a lot of fuel.

PIT-STOP Always trying to sneak in an afternoon nap.

PITTER-PATTER Like the sound of rain on the roof, this puppy's footsteps can be extremely soothing.

PIZZAZZ The exciting and attractive energy exuded by this puppy will never seem to wane.

PLATTY (PLATYPUS) Stubby legs, flat nose, water- and land-dwelling. Sound like any adorable puppy you know?

PLAYGIRL It will be hard to keep this puppy home at night.

POET A seemingly contemplative, quiet and sensitive puppy.

POGO Up and down the stairs, in and out the door, on and off the bed, this puppy bounces to and fro all day and night.

POKERFACE For the puppy who can look completely innocent even when the bed is wet and the garbage is strewn from one end of the house to the other.

POLITIX Try to avoid arguments with this puppy. They can easily ruin a meal.

POLO As in "pony." Good name for puppies destined to grow to horse size.

POM-POM Good name for a Pomeranian.

PONG *See* PING.

PONGO *See* POGO.

POOCH *See* DOG *in Chapter 1.*

POOKIE An affectionate name for an affectionate pup.

POP In his own jovial way this puppy runs the household.

PORKCHOP *See* BACON.

PORKER Is your puppy a little plump around the edges?

PORSCHE *See* MERCEDES.

PORTLY It will be hard to convince the veterinarian that this pup doesn't get table scraps.

PRECIOUS No matter how much garbage and mud this puppy gets into she will always be your precious babykins.

PRESIDENT For a puppy who will at least think he has control of the house.

PRETTIPAWS Just wait till she starts cuttin' some rug, literally.

PRETTY Beauty is in the eye of the beholder. Good name for a Bulldog, French Bulldog, Mastiff, Pug or any other dog deemed more beautiful on the inside.

PRETTY BABY *See* PRETTY.

PRETZEL Like all pups who love to chase their tail, their contortionist antics make this name appropriate.

PRIMA DONNA The world revolves around this puppy, or so she thinks. She might just be right.

PRINCESS Her stately grace and conventional beauty show signs of royalty.

PRISSY For a puppy who walks with her nose in the air. Maybe she is just smelling the flowers.

PRODIGY Nothing like a little pressure at an early age.

PROFESSOR Others have a lot to learn from this pup who will pass obedience school with flying colors.

PUDDING Good for a puppy whose chocolate brown or creamy vanilla coat brings to mind this dessert.

PUDDLES This one, not bothered by water, usually takes the quickest route through puddles: the middle.

PUDGE *See* PORTLY.

PUDGETTE A smaller version of PUDGE.

PUFFBALL There must be a puppy in there somewhere.

PUGNOSE Appropriate for a Pug or any shortfaced dog.

PUMPKIN There must be a Cinderella story behind this puppy.

PUNK An attitude check might occasionally be in order for the owner of this puppy.

PROFESSOR

PUPPY A generic name for the generic-brand fanatic.

PUTT-PUTT A short-legged pup will wear this name well.

QANTAS An Australian name for a puppy who wraps himself around your neck like a koala.

QUEEN BEE This demanding little one will love a crowd and plenty of catering to.

QUICHE Real men don't eat it, but you won't be able to keep this pup away from it.

QUICK *See* QUICKSILVER.

QUICKSILVER Built for speed. Good name for a Greyhound.

QUIRK A tiny pup with many idiosyncracies.

RADAR Nothing will get past this pup. Very alert. Great name for a Pointer or English Springer Spaniel.

RAGDOLL This good listener has taken the place of your old one. She's even fun to dress up occasionally.

RAGE This puppy will love to party . . . on your bed, with your shoes, even in the refrigerator if he or she can find a way.

RAGING BULL A perfect name for your punchy Boxer or pushy Bulldog.

RAGMOP *See* DUSTMOP.

RAGS Good for a mixed-breed dog, who loves you with or without riches.

RAGTIME *See* FLAPPER.

RAGU A chunky little pup who's always good to have around the kitchen.

RAIDER If the refrigerator looks a bit empty, maybe it has something to do with your newest family member.

RAIN *See* PITTER-PATTER.

RAINBOW This puppy is a living testament to the myth that "there is a pot of gold at the end of every rainbow." Your rainbow and gold are all wrapped in the same adorable canine package.

RAISIN Good name for a Chinese Shar-Pei or Bulldog.

RAMBO A gutsy, crafty pup who might make coming home dangerous. You never know what you will find when you open the door, especially if you did not properly puppy-proof the house before you left.

RANGER Your home will be well tended to with this puppy's territorial instincts.

RAVEN Good for a black-coated dog.

RAWHIDE This pup's favorite toy makes your favorite name.

RAZZ A bundle of surprises, this one may think there is no limit to your patience.

RAZZMATAZZ Don't let the confusion this pup causes in your life detract from his or her dazzling personality.

REBEL This puppy will be happiest when stirring things up.

RED or **REDHEAD** Good name for any dog whose coat is any shade of red.

REEBOK A tireless puppy who will always have his or her running paws on.

REPO A rescue puppy.

REUBEN According to this pup, a sandwich will do just fine for lunch.

RHAPSODY Improvising around the house will be a great source of entertainment for this irregularly composed pup.

RHINESTONE This puppy responds to a rhythm that is a little bit country and a little bit rock. A decorative, rhinestone collar is a must.

RHINO Although usually relaxed and slow, if annoyed this dog will dutifully stand his or her ground.

RIDER Don't forget his helmet.

RIFFRAFF For a puppy who causes a bit of commotion around the house.

RINGLEADER Either your children or the other animals in the house will be greatly influenced by this puppy.

RIPPLE Good name for a Chinese Shar-Pei or Bulldog.

RITZ or RITZY Posh? Ostentatious? Luxurious? Is this the type of life your dog will lead?

ROACH See CUCARACHA *in Chapter 1.*

ROCK Good name for a strong, solid dog; possibly a Rottweiler or a Bull Terrier.

ROCKER This puppy's nightlife may take a bit of getting used to.

ROCKET This little combustion chamber is easily ignited by any of the words from his or her extensive vocabulary, such as "ride, walk, park, treat," or maybe even "kitty."

RODEO This discerning puppy will walk only the finest streets.

ROGUE A scoundrel of a puppy who will add some mischievous pleasure to your life.

ROLLS See MERCEDES.

RONDEAU A literary pup whose every bark matters.

ROO (KANGAROO) This puppy's legs seem to have springs on them.

ROOSTER For the puppy who thoroughly enjoys waking you at the crack of dawn.

ROOT BEER Effervescence comes naturally for this puppy.

ROSARITA A little rose.

ROSEBUD Comical name for an "aromatic" dog.

ROSEY William Shakespeare wrote, "A rose by any other name would smell as sweet." As is the case with a lovable puppy by this name.

ROTTEN "Spoiled" or "dirty," either way the name is likely to suit your new puppy.

ROVER This endearing name for the family pet was probably derived from the word's original meaning, "a wanderer or roamer." Hats off to the special person who brought a stray in off the street and loved him so much that his name became a classic.

ROWDY A bit hard to control at times but definitely worth the effort. This was the name of the first Alaskan Malamute registered with the AKC, in 1935.

ROYAL This imperially noble puppy will have no qualms adjusting him- or herself to your more modest standard of living.

RUBY *See* Red.

RUFF Comical name for a Basenji.

RUFFIAN A playfully boisterous puppy.

RUFFLES A frilly puppy whose feathers are easily ruffled if he or she is not given plenty of attention.

RUFUS A common and endearing name for a well-loved puppy. This name was probably derived from the reddish color of many dogs' coats. It was the name of the first Field Spaniel registered with the AKC, in 1894.

RUGRAT Fitting name for a heavy-coat Toy dog, who probably could use some grooming.

RUNNER A farm, or lots of space, is needed to appease this energetic puppy.

RUNT Comical name for a big dog. *See* BABY.

RUSTY *See* RED.

SAGA Long, detailed accounts of this puppy's cute behavior can become boring to some, however true dog lovers will never grow weary.

SAILOR Finally, in you he has a port he can call home.

SAKE Warm-spirited.

SALSA Having much spice and energy.

SALTY Seasoned with the smell of the ocean in his or her coat.

SAND RAT Sounds like you have a real beach dog.

SANDMAN This puppy looks extremely peaceful when he sleeps, which is often.

SANTA FE This puppy's style is the newest trend, but he or she won't be your passing fancy.

SAPPHIRE She already shines brighter than you thought possible.

SARASOTA A puppy with this name might add life to a previously retired household.

SARGE Good name for a German Shepherd Dog.

SASQUATCH The Indian name for "Bigfoot." You're not quite sure where he came from, or what he's made of, but you love him just the same.

SASSAFRAS Does this puppy have a more "energetic flavor" than you expected?

SASSY Lively and very independent.

SATIN A smooth, lustrous coat is worn by this well-groomed puppy.

SAUCE or **SAUCY** In contemporary slang this describes something or someone who looks good, like any and all adorable female puppies.

SAUSAGE The contortionist wiggles this puppy will make when he or she greets you at the door are demonstrative of this name. Also good for dogs who are literally shaped like sausages.

SAVAGE A comical name for a harmless and very sweet-looking puppy.

SCAMPER When attempting to run this puppy's back legs move in hopping unison like a scampering rabbit.

SCARBOROUGH What an affair puppyhood can turn out to be.

SCHMOO "Oh what a cute little schmoo." This word quite possibly represents the cuddliest dog in the world.

SCHMOOZE Kissing up to you will be one of this puppy's best tricks.

SCHOONER Very much a water pup who will handle waves with graceful poise.

SCHWEPPES *See* Root Beer.

SCINTILLA For the tiniest pup around. Good for any Toy-breed pup.

SCOOTER A pup known to chase them as they go by could have earned this name, as well as one who simply moves quite quickly.

SCOTCH A smooth Scottish blend such as a Scottish Terrier.

SCOUNDREL A puppy with this name may look a bit rough around the edges. A good bath and clean bed can work wonders.

SCOUT This curious pup has the ability to dig up all kinds of surprises.

SCRAPPY The ancestry of this dog is completely unknown.

SCRUFFY See SCRAPPY.

SCRUMPTIOUS For a yummy-looking puppy.

SCUBA This pup loves to dive, whether it is in a pool, ocean surf or food dish. For his safety, be sure someone is around when he does.

SCUD Incoming puppy!

SEABREEZE A rejuvenating puppy whose playful antics will be infectious.

SEAL Good for a pup with a loud bark, a funny waddle in his or her walk and a shiny, short-haired, black coat, like a black-and-tan Doberman Pinscher, black Labrador, Manchester Terrier or Rottweiler.

SERENADE A puppy with this name will have a tendency to "sing," but his timing is rotten.

SHADOW For a puppy who is always right behind you.

SHAMROCK The luck of the Irish was with you when you found this puppy.

SHARKEY A respected and revered pup in the neighborhood and local park. Good for feisty characters like Jack Russell Terriers or Miniature Pinschers.

SHARP Good for quick-learning pups who will find obedience school an easy read.

SHE-DEVIL Bulging eyes, frantically wagging tail, tongue hanging out . . . yes, you have a possessed puppy.

SHEIK Try hand-feeding this puppy grapes or rocking him to sleep to keep him happy.

SHENANIGANS An endlessly mischievous and high-spirited puppy, whose idea of a trick hardly merits a treat.

SHERIFF Good for a German Shepherd Dog puppy who will probably grow into his protective and arbitrative demeanor.

SHIM SHIM SHIREE A puppy who loves to "sing."

SHOELESS This puppy will take a toll on your wardrobe.

SHOOTER This pup shoots around the house as if he or she owns the place, and guess what? He or she does.

SHORTY, SHORTCAKE or SHORTSTACK
This name might give your Chihuahua, Dachshund or Miniature Pinscher a complex. Comical name for a large dog.

SHOTGUN For the puppy who will insist on sitting in the front passenger seat.

SHOWBOAT This puppy, with an inflated ego, will spend much time upstaging you.

SHOWOFF This egotistical pup might be prone to stealing other puppies' Frisbees or tennis balls.

SHRAPNEL Good for a pup who has the uncanny ability to shake himself dry in all the wrong places, like your living room.

SHREDDER This puppy either loves to chew or is a ski aficionado.

SIDEWAYS For the puppy whose bow legs give him a cute sideways strut.

SILHOUETTE A pup whose narrow build makes him or her appear one-dimensional, like the Borzoi, Italian Greyhound or Whippet.

SILKY What else but a Silky Terrier?

SILVERSPOON Conventional toys and food might be a problem for this overindulged, eccentric pup.

SIN Temptation is this pup's biggest flaw. Also an abbreviation for Cinnamon.

SINGER This puppy's serenades may go too far . . . into the morning hours.

SISSY Good name for dogs from breeds that are thought to possess aggressive tendencies.

SIX TOES Good name for a puppy with an extra dew claw.

SKEDADDLE A short leash might be imperative for this wandering pup.

SKEEDER Slang for mosquito.

SKIDDER A pup whose momentum occasionally requires him to put on the brakes and skid to a stop.

SKIPPY A light-footed puppy with a spring in his or her walk.

SKITTLES Good for the coy but capricious kind of pup.

SKY A serene, relaxing pup with blue eyes. Good for a Siberian Husky.

SKY HAWK This one requires a spacious yard and like most dogs will probably circle his sleeping place before lying down.

SKYROCKET The ability to jump low fences in a single bound will make this name appropriate for your pup.

SLATE A compact, gray pup.

SLICKER Pleading eyes are a front and an asset for this swindler who can sucker you into giving him a treat whenever he chooses.

SLIPPERS Oh how sweet. Look what puppy did to your new shoes. Time to start putting things where they belong.

SLOBBER-PUSS Good for any dog with a tendency to drool.

SLOTH This little pup would rather be carried than put on a leash.

SLUGGER This brash half-pint hit a home run when he found you.

SLY With a name like this you might want to hide your favorite shoes or trinkets.

SMASHER Keep this pup away from your favorite crystal.

SMOKEY An ash-colored pup, such as a Weimaraner.

SMOOCHER Kisses will be lavishly bestowed by a slobbering puppy with this name.

SNACKER Between, before and after meals, this puppy will willingly devour treats.

SNAGGLETOOTH Although the teeth might not be perfect this name for him or her certainly is.

SNAP your fingers and this one comes running.

SNARL This often disgruntled pup will have no problems voicing his or her demands.

SNEAKERS Good for dogs who love to run, such as an Italian Greyhound or a rescued track Greyhound.

SNICKERS For a puppy who seems to smile at you.

SNIFFER A persnickety pup whose sniffing can often be misinterpreted for snootiness.

SNIFFLES A wheezing little pup known for musical breathing, like the Bulldog or Pug.

SNIFTER *See* BRANDY.

SNO-PEA Good for a Bichon Frise, Maltese, white Miniature or Toy Poodle or West Highland White Terrier.

SNOCAP Good name for a Dandie Dinmont Terrier, Bichon Frise or Chinese Crested.

SNOOGYBEAR A cuter version of SNOOKS.

SNOOKS Sounds like a name a grandparent would create.

SNOOKUMS An even cuter version of SNOOKS.

SNOOPER A curious puppy who might get him or herself into trouble every now and then.

SNOOTY For a puppy who carries his or her nose proudly in the air.

SNORTER This puppy's snuffling noises add character.

SNOW, SNOWBALL or SNOWFLAKE Good for a Bichon Frise, Maltese, white Poodle, Samoyed or any puppy, white or not, who loves to play in the snow.

SNOW BUNNY

SNUGGLES

SNOWBERRY A pretty, evocative name for a little dog you can share a winter walk with.

SNOWBUNNY His or her bouncy stride in the first snow might make this name appropriate.

SNOWMAN Good for snow-loving pups, such as Siberian Huskies, Alaskan Malamutes, Newfoundlands, Saint Bernards or Samoyeds.

SNUFFLES Puppies with constricted breathing tend to snuffle their way through life: Chinese Shar-Peis, Bulldogs, Boston Terriers and Pugs.

SNUGGLES or **SNUGGLE-PUSS** For a puppy who insists on snuggling in your lap, no matter how large he or she is. Funny name for a big, tough-looking dog.

SOCKS There is a good chance that this one's favorite pastime is emptying your sock drawer.

SOLO This loner pup will make you his or her one and only.

SOLSTICE For puppies whose birthdays fall on June or December 22.

SONATA See MELODY.

SORBET A little pat on this puppy's head before your main course will invariably help both of you better enjoy your entrée.

SORCERER or **SORCERESS** Somehow this puppy will manage to open the locked doggie door, get into the closed garbage can and find leftovers when the refrigerator is closed. Better find a way to confound the magic!

SOUTHERN COMFORT This "down home" puppy will add a bit of taste and comfort to your life.

SOUTHPAW For a puppy who clumsily tilts to the left when he or she runs.

SPADES *See* BLACKIE.

SPAGHETTI Good for pups who will sport corded coats at maturity, like the Komondor or Puli.

SPAM Good for a pup who is a combination of a few indiscernible breeds.

SPARKEY or **SPARKLE** For a puppy with that unmistakable happy glint in his or her eye.

SPARKPLUG A self-starter. This punchy little pup will have you walking him or her in your sleep.

SPARROW Good name for a Whippet.

SPECS Appropriate for a Dalmatian puppy, yet humorous for a dog marked in such a way that he or she appears to be wearing glasses, such as a Keeshond.

SPEEDY You might want to keep a leash handy if you plan on raising a pup with this name.

SPELLBINDER Good name for a puppy whose melting eyes can convince you to do just about anything: walks, treats, rides . . .

SPICY A puppy with this name will probably add some flavor to your life.

SPIDER Appropriate name for a gangly-legged puppy, such as your Doberman Pinscher, Great Dane or Greyhound pup. Just remember—he won't always be that way.

SPIKE Good name for a Chinese Crested or Rhodesian Ridgeback due to his or her physical trait. *See* MOHAWK *in Chapter 1.*

SPINNER Chasing his or her tail is characteristic of this pup.

SPIRIT This puppy is full of it.

SPITFIRE For a puppy with some fire behind her eyes. Maybe she is just looking for a Frisbee.

SPLASH Good name for a water-loving puppy such as a Labrador or Golden Retriever, or for any puppy who insists on shaking when being given a bath.

SPOOKY This timid, paranoid critter will sometimes run from his or her own shadow.

SPORT *See* OL' SPORT.

SPOT Perfect for a solid-colored dog.

SPRITE *See* SPUNKY.

SPUDS What other than a Bull Terrier?

SPUMANTI This little Italian Greyhound or Neapolitan Mastiff puppy will add color and flavor to any owner's life.

SPUNKY A shortage of energy is not one of this puppy's problems.

SPY For the puppy who always seems to be on your heels.

SPYRO *See* GYRO.

SQUAT *See* STUBBY.

SQUEAKY Good name for a Basenji, who squeaks or chortles rather than barks.

SQUID A funny-looking, water-loving pup.

SQUIRT Good name for a little pup with a big bark.

STAR This beautiful puppy belongs in pictures, but don't they all?

STARDUST or **STARLIGHT** A romantic puppy with eyes that glisten like stars and a coat the color of evening shade.

STARGAZER Good name for a puppy who loves to watch the night sky. Is he or she looking for *Canis Major*?

STARLET A real drama queen. For a puppy who knows how to ham it up in order to get what she wants.

STELLAR The "stellar" performances this puppy will give will definitely be conversation pieces at your dinner parties.

STERLING Only the best for this and all puppies.

STINKER or **STINKER BELLE** A bit of a mischievous pup.

STINKY This scruffy little pup has an aura all her or his own.

STOLI A power-packed little pup or one of Russian descent, like a Borzoi.

STONEY This befuddled pup will love to watch life go by.

STORM or **STORMY** A whirlwind of a puppy whose tempestuous manner will leave your household in constant disarray.

STOWAWAY This puppy picked you.

STRAY Good for the pup who was lost but now is found—a STRAY in name only.

STRUDEL A sweet little German puppy, such as a Dachshund or Miniature Pinscher.

STARLET

STORMY

STUBBY or **STUBBLES** It is amazing that those short, little legs can actually move this hefty puppy.

STUMP Good name for a dog with a short, stubby or docked tail.

SUGAR The sweetest pup of them all. This was the name of the sea lion in the Marilyn Monroe movie *Some Like It Hot*; therefore this is a good name for a black Labrador or a black-and-tan Doberman Pinscher.

SUGAR-PLUM This sweet puppy can be a little messy at times.

SUGARBABY Good name for an incredibly spoiled puppy.

SUGARBAKER A sweet puppy who loves to hang out in the kitchen, just in case anything happens to drop.

SUNDOWN This puppy's warmth and glow leave you with a lasting impression.

SUNKISS This one will bathe you with her warm morning kisses.

SUNNYBROOK This puppy needs to live on a farm so she has plenty of space to run.

SUNRISE Just like the morning sun, this one lets you know when it is time to wake up.

SUNSHINE She or he makes you happy when skies are gray.

SUPERTRAMP This king or queen of tramps will have no problem making friends at the park—with you along, of course.

SUSHI A puppy with this name will always leave you hungry for more of his or her affection.

SWAMI This spiritually enlightened puppy might just teach you a thing or two.

SWAMPY An avid gatherer, there is no telling what slimy little gifts this one will drag in.

SWEET CHEEKS For a puppy who wiggles while she walks.

SWEET PEA This name has a Southern twang to it. Good name for a Redbone Coonhound.

SWEETHEART, SWEETIE or **SWEETNESS** A puppy with this name will give lots of wet kisses, especially on Valentine's Day. We recommend lots of toys and treats to keep her happy.

SWIZZLE A puppy with this name must have some contortionist abilities.

SYMPHONY This grunting, wheezing little puppy will be music to your ears.

SYNERGY If you work with this puppy enough, he or she is bound to grow up to be a strong, healthy dog who will undoubtedly leave a mark on society.

T.L.C. Tender loving care is what this pup will give at all times.

T.N.T. This pup is a living testament that big things come in small packages.

TABOO Although this puppy is not forbidden to be touched, a name like this might help you keep him or her all to yourself.

TAFFY A sweet, sticky little pup.

TAG A playful pup whose favorite game might just be what his or her name depicts.

TAHITI A puppy with this name could easily get used to napping in hammocks and being served delicacies as the days drift by. Then again, this probably would not be any different from his or her present life.

TALAHACHE It is best to keep a puppy with this name away from bridges.

TALLYHO Just a jingle of the car keys and this pup will know it is time to go for a ride.

TAMAHTO It's all in how you say the name.

TANGO Take this puppy to Paris and watch him dance for the joys of doggie freedom.

TANK A puppy with this name will be convinced she or he can go through closed doors.

TANNER While most puppies are finding a shady spot to relax this pup will be looking for the best place to sun.

TAR An old-fashioned name often used during the nineteenth century. Most suitable for black or dark dogs.

TARBABY It seems everything sticks to this innocent little puppy: mud, drool, food . . .

TARGA *See* MERCEDES.

TAROT This mystic puppy holds the cards to your bright puppy-rearing future.

TARRAGON This puppy enhances your flavor for life.

TATTERS Good for Komondors, Old English Sheepdogs, Pulis or any other breed with a similar coat.

TATTLETALE This puppy will be the first to flee the scene of a crime and the first to blame the cat.

TATTOO This puppy will leave a permanent imprint on your heart, and your house.

TAURUS Stubbornness will be this puppy's most prominent quality.

TAXI You never know what you'll get when you yell this name.

TAZ Short for Tasmanian devil. A puppy with this name will seem to wreak havoc wherever he or she goes, but isn't he or she adorable while doing it?

TAZER Don't let puppyhood stun you too much.

TEACUP Henry James wrote, "... there are few hours in life more agreeable than the hour dedicated to the ceremony known as afternoon tea." This is certainly true if you share it with a puppy. Good name for a Toy Poodle or any other tiny dog.

TEASE or **TEASER** A coy little puppy, who is in actuality a sucker for affection.

TENNESSEE This pup loves a good country tune and occasionally will chime in with a well-timed howl.

TERRA-COTTA Tiled floors are convenient for puppy raising.

TERROR Although this pup might seem a bit destructive at first, a little positive training and a lot of love can make a real difference.

TESTAROSSA Built for speed, this pup will turn heads everywhere.

THAI Spicy and exotic. This puppy will keep you intrigued.

THORN or **THISTLE** Spiky little hairs protect this rose of a pup from a host of mishaps. Good name for any small, harsh-coated terrier, Wirehaired Dachshund or Petit Basset Griffon Vendeen.

THUDPAW Appropriate name for a puppy whose paws are so large that he or she can't seem to control them.

THUNDER Sets the stage for LIGHTNING.

THYME *See* TARRAGON.

TIE-DYE Great name for a brindle puppy.

TIGER A prowling, mystifying pup whose bark is worse than his bite. Hold that tiger.

TINKER One who repairs household items and experiments with machines. With a puppy like this, closing cupboards and closets makes sense.

TINKERTOY This restless pup needs plenty of toys to experiment with, for reasons given in the previous entry.

TINKLE BELL This name is a takeoff on Peter Pan's friendly little ball of light. It's for the puppy who leaves "shimmering pools" wherever she goes.

TINSEL This one, despite his or her name, is all he or she is cracked up to be.

TINY Good for the smallest puppy of the litter, or for one who promises to grow out of the name, such as a Great Dane or Irish Wolfhound.

TIPSY Equilibrium will not be one of this pup's greater abilities.

TISSOT A precise pup who will run through his commands like clockwork.

TIZZY or TIZZ The slightest alteration in her daily routine can throw this puppy into confusion. Don't skip one minute of her walk time.

TOAD This fat little pup will sit around a lot, like a bump on a log. One kiss might just bring you a prince.

TOM-TOM *See* DRUMMER.

TOMAHAWK A few relentless cries and this pup is off and running.

TOOTER For the puppy who loves to toot his own horn.

TOOTSIE A classic name that brightens any dog's life.

TORNADO Look at him go. The best thing to do is simply to stay out of this pup's path.

TOUCHÉ A sly pup who will outsmart you whenever you aren't looking.

TOYBOX This pup deserves the biggest one on the block.

TRAILBLAZER *See* PATHFINDER.

TREAT A puppy like this won't mind doing a trick for his treat. Good name for the second puppy in the household could be TRICK.

TREKKY For an addicted *Star Trek* watcher and follower, this is a terrific puppy name. Completely logical!

TRICKY A clever pup who will be chock-full of surprises.

TRINKET At times this puppy is rather hard to find. Good for a puppy from one of the Toy breeds.

TRIP This puppy seems to be in his own world ... until you ring the dinner bell.

TRIXIE The feminine version of TRICKY.

TROJAN Good name for a dog destined to grow the size of a horse.

TROLL This gargoylesque pup will like nothing better than bravely guarding your treasures, and he probably looks far more menacing than he is.

TROPICANA Appropriate name for a puppy of exotic heritage with a preference for basking in the sun.

TROUBADOUR Love is the main theme of this poetic puppy's life.

TROUBLE Cute name for a very calm puppy.

TROUPER Good with children, he or she will put up with just about anything.

TRUFFLEHUNTER Usually the task of locating truffles is assigned to a trained pig, but your dog will do fine. Good name for a dog who tends to eat anything you put in front of him or her.

TRUFFLES A delicacy among humans and dogs. Spoiling your baby at an early age, are you?

TUBBO (also TUBBY or TUBS) An affectionate name for a chubby little pup.

TUFFY An always popular name for an always adorable puppy.

TUGBOAT Good name for a Bulldog due to its "chugging" noises, otherwise known as breathing.

TUNA This puppy's intentions smell a bit fishy when he is hovering about the refrigerator.

TUNDRA A puppy with this name can brave about any climate, but he won't appreciate you testing his limits.

TURBO All we need—a puppy with accelerated speed.

TURKEY This puppy will gobble up anything you put in front of his or her face.

TUTTI-FRUTTI How easily this name rolls off the tongue.

TWERP A miniature, mischievous pup who opens his mouth a little more often than you might like.

TWINKIE A yummy name for a yummy pup.

TWINKLE A sparkle will be forever present in this puppy's eyes.

TWISTER A game-playing puppy who will never cease to amaze you with his contortionist antics.

TYCOON A puppy with an overly territorial tendency to monopolize larger playing boundaries.

URCHIN Good name for a harsh-coated dog with an "in your face" attitude.

VAGABOND This vagabond puppy's wandering days are over.

VALENTINE You'll never want another.

VANILLA Good for a white or cream-colored dog. As a name for a second dog in the family try adding a little SAUCE.

VEGGIE *See* COUCH POTATO.

VELCRO A puppy with this name will probably stick very close to your side.

VELVET Royal material, just like your puppy.

VIOLET Your little dogtooth violet is a rare creature.

VIPER Quick, sharp and ready to strike, but only at his or her food dish.

VISA This puppy will be well traveled and schooled, and widely accepted.

VIXEN This puppy might be more than you bargained for.

VOYAGER Don't leave this puppy at home. He would love to go anywhere with you.

VROOM VROOM This puppy is just revving up. Wait till he takes off.

WACKY and crazy is a good way to describe this puppy.

WADDLES Hopefully his or her legs will continue to grow.

WAG-A-LOT For a puppy who wags his whole body along with his tail.

WAGS That tail should be a registered weapon.

WALLFLOWER This puppy likes to do things her own way.

WALRUS With tusklike teeth, flipperesque legs and over-grown whiskers, this puppy will make quite a production out of movement.

WARLOCK *See* STREGA *in Chapter 1.*

WARRIOR *See* NINJA *in Chapter 1.*

WARTHOG *See* PIGGY *in Chapter 1.*

WEB You've been caught in this puppy's web of affection.

WHIRLWIND A frenzied furball who will leave dust and destruction everywhere.

WHISKEY Puppy behavior can be a shock at first, but once you become accustomed to it it's hard to live without.

WHISPER or **WHISPERWIND** Subtlety, elegance and soft-spokenness are traits held by this puppy.

WHOOPIE This exclamation of happiness and celebration is exactly what you will be yelling when your new puppy comes home.

WIGGLES For the puppy who simply will not sit still.

WILD THING This puppy will make your heart sing.

WILDWOOD A lover of the great outdoors.

WIMPY Good name for a large, strong, slightly overbearing dog.

WINDJAMMER On top deck, with wind and water whipping at his coat, is where you will find this sea dog.

WINDY "Flighty" and "restless" describe this sweet puppy.

WINK This puppy will always make eyes at you.

WISEGUY This one likes to talk back.

WIZARD With one wave of his paw this puppy can drastically change the surroundings.

WIZKID The smartest puppy on the block.

WOODSTOCK A dropout of the sixties. This puppy embodies the serenity and playful youthfulness of a monumental period.

WOODWIND A classic puppy named after a classic type of instrument.

WOOF For a puppy whose bark will be worse than his bite.

WOOLLY MAMMOTH Very large and very shaggy are adjectives that describe this puppy.

WRANGLER This wrestling pooch will be in heaven if you roll around with him for a while.

YABBA-DABBA-DOO Used as an exclamation of excitement by Fred Flintstone in the 1970s cartoon "The Flintstones." With all the things puppies have to get excited about you'll have quite a vocal pup on your hands with this name.

YAHOO Resembling YABBA-DABBA-DOO in terms of a puppy's yelps of glee.

YANKEE Poodle Dandee!

YO-YO Up and down this puppy goes. Where he or she lands nobody knows.

YOU TOO For a puppy who will need commands repeated because he or she will always think you are addressing the other dog of the household.

YUMMY Looking so luscious you just want to gobble her up.

ZIPPITY DO DA Zippity Ay, my oh my what a wonderful . . . puppy.

ZODIAC A temperamental puppy who will seem to be driven by something other than your commands.

ZOMBIE It will take a while to awaken this puppy from his or her naps.

ZOOEY A puppy with this name would be just as happy living in a zoo; however, your house probably isn't much of a stretch.

ZOOM ZOOM *See* SPEEDY.

ZZZ Pronounced "zees." A puppy with this name will be prone to extensive napping.

3

Names Fit for a King, Queen or Pauper

THIS CHAPTER is what leaders, heroes, gods, stars and puppies are made of. In it you will find suggestions for names as memorable and timeless as the puppies wearing them. Whether your puppy is as territorial as Napoleon or has the underbite of Brando or the aura of Aurora, you will find plenty of names to help immortalize him or her.

ABERCROMBIE A well-groomed and stylish puppy deserves this name.

ACHILLES The hero of Homer's *Iliad* who had one small, but mortal, weakness, his vulnerable heel. A puppy with this name could have a weakness for any number of things: cookies, rides, walks, pillows or, of course, affection.

ADONIS The name of a youth in Greek mythology loved by Aphrodite because of his great beauty. This was also the name of the first dog registered in the AKC stud book, an English Setter, in 1878.

AESOP From *The Fables of Aesop,* in which animals sometimes appear in semi-human form and teach the reader a lesson. A puppy with this name might move as slowly as a tortoise, but his diligence is to be admired.

AJAX A Greek hero in the Trojan War who commits suicide after losing the armor of Achilles to Odysseus. A puppy with this name might have the classic look of an ancient Greek or Roman dog, such as a Greyhound or Neapolitan Mastiff.

ALADDIN A puppy with this name will do his best to make sure all your wishes are granted.

ALFALFA A mischievous rascal of a puppy whose trademark might be a couple of hairs standing upright on his head.

ALI This living legend flies like a butterfly, but hardly stings like a bee. A natural name choice for a Boxer.

ALI BABA The stains on your carpet will not fly away, no matter what this magical puppy believes.

ALOYSIUS A famous Germanic warrior. Good name for a German Shepherd Dog.

AMOS Like the chimpanzee so named, your puppy probably thinks he is part monkey and part human. *See* GOOCH *in Chapter 2.*

ANAIS Much like the American writer Anais Nin (1903–1977), this pup is a highly imaginative, psychologically in-depth one, who probably has the aroma of fine perfume.

ANASTASIA Convenient memory loss tends to appear when obedience commands are administered to this puppy who will rarely remember her name.

ANDROMEDA In Greek mythology she was rescued from a sea monster by her husband Perseus. A puppy with this name should have delicate, feminine features; Whippets often answer the description.

APOLLO The Greek mythological god of the sun, prophecy, music, medicine and poetry; or any young man of great physical beauty. Here is a name with a lot of built-in expectations.

ARCHIE The lead character in the Bob Montana comic strip "Archie" (1958). A puppy with this name is definitely a redhead. *See* RED *in Chapter 2.*

ARES The Greek mythological god of war. Keeping this pup in line will be a constant battle.

ARGUS The hound of Odysseus.

ARGUS In Greek mythology he was a giant with one hundred eyes who was made guardian of Io and later slain by Hermes. He is known as an alert, watchful guardian. Doberman Pinschers, like the giant, are said to be so alert that they must have eyes in the back of their heads due to their ability to catch the slightest movement.

ARIEL In medieval literature this character was portrayed as a water spirit, however in Shakespeare's *The Tempest* she was a spirit of the air who was required to use magic in order to help Prospero. Whether on land or water this puppy will have the right spell to make you feel good.

ARISTOTLE This puppy will beg to differ with his namesake's quote that states, ". . . man alone of the animals is furnished with faculty of language" (*The Politics of Aristotle*). You probably have a very vocal pup on your hands.

ARMANI For the high-fashion, well-groomed puppy.

ARMSTRONG Daniel Louis Armstrong, "Satchmo" (1900–1971), strongly influenced the development of jazz, including its rise in soloism. A puppy with this name will have rhythm and be a bit independent.

ASTRO This dog name was made famous by the cartoon dog in "The Jetsons." He, probably like your pooch, was able to communicate his every thought to his owners.

ATHENA In Greek mythology she was the goddess of wisdom and the arts. Obedience school should be a cinch for this brilliant puppy.

ATLAS In Greek mythology he was a titan condemned to support the heavens upon his shoulders, like a brooding, pensive pup who acts as if the weight of the world is on his shoulders.

ATTICUS Titus Pomponius (109–32 B.C.) adapted this name as his surname due to his long residence in Athens. Your puppy should already have adopted your surname. No matter how long he or she has resided with you this puppy is a permanent resident.

ATTILA The King of the Huns, A.D. 453. He was a savage, but at times just, ruler. This puppy will usually know what proper behavior is; however, it probably isn't wise to take his bone away from him.

AUGUSTUS This first Roman emperor Augustus Caesar (63 B.C.–A.D. 14) was the grandnephew of Julius Caesar, whose death he avenged by defeating Brutus and Cassius. A puppy with this name will be loyal to any deserving owner.

AURORA Roman mythological goddess of the dawn. Appropriate for an early riser who will take the place of your alarm clock.

AVIS A dynasty of Portuguese rulers. Bossiness runs in this puppy's family. Good name for a Portuguese Water Dog, naturally.

BABA (MAYOR) "Don't worry, be happy" is a motto of this political figure that this puppy apparently lives for.

BABE Short for the legendary baseball great Babe Ruth. You hit a home run when you brought home this baby.

BABS Nickname for singer Barbra Streisand. Good name for an Afghan Hound, Borzoi or Saluki.

BACCHUS The god of winemaking. Good name for a mahogany-colored puppy, as well as one that is still too clumsy to be considered sober.

BACH If you're into this great composer, you might want to name your Dachshund or Rottweiler after him.

BALBOA In the feature film *Rocky* the lead character, Rocky Balboa, owned a Bullmastiff.

BAM-BAM This pudgy, bone-carrying character from the seventies cartoon "The Flintstones" probably resembles your pup, if not in his affection for bones then in his or her noise-making ability.

BAMBI Good name for a gangly, long-legged puppy or for a dog of uncommon grace at maturity.

BANQUO A Scottish nobleman in William Shakespeare's tragedy *Macbeth*. Good name for any Scottish breed.

BARBARINO *See* SWEATHOG.

BART You have a modern-day Dennis the Menace on your hands.

BARTHOLOMEW A saint and one of the apostles. This puppy would follow you to the ends of the earth. His or her actions are virtuous and loyalty instinctual.

BASHFUL A shy, quiet puppy.

BAXTER Named after the English nonconformist chaplain and scholar Richard Baxter (1615–1691), this very wise pup will have a hard time doing as others do . . . or say.

BEAUREGARD Pierre Gustave Beauregard (1818–1893) was a Confederate general stationed for some time in St. Bernard Parish, Louisiana. This Saint Bernard pup will usually be the leader of the pack.

BEETHOVEN If you like his music, honor your Weimaraner or Schnauzer accordingly.

BEETLEJUICE For the puppy whose antics will make your head spin.

BEN After the famous grizzly bear, Gentle Ben. *See* BEAR *in Chapter 2.*

BENJI A shaggy mutt with this name was star of the movie *Benji* and has resulted in countless namesakes since.

BESSIE This was the name of the first Dalmatian registered with the AKC, in 1888.

BETTY BOOP Good name for a Boston Terrier who, during the 1920s, like this black-and-white comic strip character, was all the rage.

BIKO For the puppy who will not be afraid to stand up for what he believes in.

BISMARCK Leon Bismarck was an American jazz composer and cornetist. Good name for a musically inclined puppy who breaks out into an occasional song and dance.

BLITZEN A bringer of joy and good cheer, this little puppy will make every day seem like Christmas.

BOCCACCIO Italian poet, storyteller and humanist Giovanni Boccaccio (1313–1375) devoted the latter portion of his life to critical works in anthropology, biology and mythology. A puppy with this name will leave an indelible mark on its people's lives.

BOGART or **BOGIE** Humphrey Bogart (1899–1957), American actor, played many roles as a tough, rather cynical hero. A puppy with this name probably has a way with women and will always come out looking like the hero.

BOND Named after the legendary Ian Fleming fictitious double agent, James Bond, this puppy knows where you hide the treats because he is forever spying on you, and of course, like Bond, he will only get better-looking with age.

BONO This puppy has got you, babe.

BOO-BOO Originally Yogi Bear's sidekick and apprentice, he's yours now.

BOONE Good name for an outdoor dog who will insist on blazing trails.

BOZ Charles Dickens's nickname. *See* DICKENS.

BRADSTREET A puppy with a head for business, but only half a head without DUN. These two know how to get the most out of their bones.

BRANDO A pup with a flair for acting, who could get you to believe anything.

BREATHLESS MAHONEY Good name for a snuffling Boston Terrier, Boxer, Bulldog, Bullmastiff or Pug.

BRONSON If this puppy does not get what he wants, he is liable to take matters into his own paws.

BRONTË Charlotte, Emily and Anne Brontë were three early nineteenth-century English sisters, novelists and poets. Good names for a three-dog household are the names of the sisters. A single, imaginative puppy deserves the name Brontë.

BRUTUS In Shakespeare's *Julius Caesar* this character assassinates Caesar. For comic relief a puppy with this name should be a harmless lap dog.

BUCK This is the name of the shaggy Briard on the television show *Married . . . with Children*.

BUCKWHEAT This little puppy is as mischievous as any of the other little rascals.

BUGSY Much like the suave mobster of the twenties, this dog has a way with women and will easily become accustomed to stealing the show.

BULLWINKLE Goofy to say the least!

BUTCH Emulating Butch Cassidy from the movie *Butch Cassidy and the Sundance Kid*, this blue-eyed pup will be a harmless troublemaker. Good name for a Siberian Husky.

BUTKUS The name of Rocky Balboa's Bullmastiff in the movie *Rocky*.

CAESAR After the reigns of Julius and Augustus Caesar this Roman family name acquired imperial character. The title was given to the Roman emperor and then reappeared as the German "kaiser" and Russian "czar." A dog with this name just might go down in history.

CAGNEY James Cagney, an American film actor accustomed to playing bad guys. This puppy will probably give a few Oscar-winning performances.

CALLOWAY Cab Calloway, the king of Hi De Ho, was an American bandleader and singer. Good name for a puppy who is rarely quiet.

CALYPSO Greek mythology gave this name to a sea nymph who delayed Odysseus on her island, Ogygia, for seven years, a short time compared to your puppy's ability to buy play time.

CAMUS Philosopher and novelist Albert Camus, 1913–1960. A puppy with this name will be intensely concerned with your well-being.

CAPONE Gangster Alfonso Capone may have been the mentor of this tenacious and fearless pup.

CARRAWAY Nick Carraway, the narrator of the F. Scott Fitzgerald novel *The Great Gatsby*, was always present when action was happening. Your puppy will probably be the one creating this action in your household instead of idly reporting on it.

CASPER Good for a dog who is forever disappearing and even better for an all-white one.

CASSIDY Butch Cassidy, Robert Leroy Parker, was a train robber and outlaw. His life was the subject of the film *Butch Cassidy and the Sundance Kid. See* BUTCH.

CASSIUS Cassius Clay, a world-renowned boxer, later changed his name to Muhammad Ali.

CHAPLIN Good name for a Basenji, who does not need to bark to make a point.

CHARLOTTE This character in E. B. White's story *Charlotte's Web* (1952) was a spider. A puppy with this name must have long, gangly, clumsy spider legs.

CHAUCER Geoffrey Chaucer, poet, lived approximately from 1343–1400. No formal training to excel is needed for a puppy with this name.

CHEKHOV Like the Russian writer and physician Anton Pavlovich Chekhov (1860–1904), this puppy has the potential to greatly influence your life.

CHEWBACCA A large, hairy, talking creature from the movie *Star Wars*, whose shaggy coat resembles that of a Briard.

CHOPIN For the puppy who prefers piano nocturnes.

CHURCHILL This name has become popular for Bulldogs due to former British Prime Minister Winston Churchill's affection for and likeness to them.

CIRCE In *The Odyssey* this mythological sorceress bewitched Ulysses and his crew and exercised her power to turn men into pigs. Your chubby porkeresque pup might have been affected by Circe's spell. *See* Piggy *in Chapter 1.*

CONFUCIUS Puppy says, "The more table scraps I get, the better I listen."

COOKIE MONSTER This Sesame Street character's habits often mirror those of all puppies.

COUSTEAU Definitely a water-loving Labrador or Newfoundland who will go to all lengths and depths to find his submerged toys.

CROCKETT For a puppy who thinks he is king of the wild frontier.

CROMWELL Oliver Cromwell, a political, military and religious leader (1599–1658). Now, his namesake is just leader of your house.

CRUSOE From Daniel Defoe's literary masterpiece, *Robinson Crusoe*, 1719, in which this hero, an English sailor, is shipwrecked and lives on a small tropical island for years with only one companion, FRIDAY. A survivalist, this puppy will make the most of any home, especially yours.

CURIOUS GEORGE This fictional monkey seemed to cause trouble wherever he went. Maybe your puppy so named can learn from the monkey's mistakes. Of course, that means you have to read all the Curious George stories to your puppy.

CURLY Good name for an exceptionally clumsy Xoloitzcuintli.

CYRANO A puppy with a good sense of humor. *See* PINOCCHIO.

DA VINCI Leonardo da Vinci (1452–1519), a Renaissance genius: painter, sculptor, architect, musician, engineer and scientist. Good name for a puppy who already accomplishes things you never dreamt possible.

DAGWOOD Named after this word for a multilayered sandwich with many fillings. Dagwood Bumstead, from the comic strip "Blondie" by Murat B. Young (1901–1973), was accustomed to making such sandwiches, sandwiches that your puppy with this name can devour in one bite.

DAISY Daisy Fay Buchanan was the heroine of the F. Scott Fitzgerald novel *The Great Gatsby*. A pup with this name will more than likely live up to her heroine's beauty and poise.

DALAI LAMA A Tibetan spiritual leader. Rumor has it that the Dalai Lama of Tibet offered Chinese emperors Lhasa Apsos as precious gifts.

DALI A puppy with this name will easily turn your home into a series of seemingly surreal scenes.

DANTE Your heart will be an inferno of love for this puppy.

DANU The mythological goddess of death and mother of the gods. A puppy with this name will oversee your house with a type of omniscient presence.

DAPHNE Derived from "Daffodil," one of the rarer flowers, like your puppy.

DARTH VADER The local black-coated bully.

DASHER The leader of the pack, whether it be dogs or reindeer.

DEGAS A puppy with this name will be noticed for her graceful balletic poses and sculptured poise.

DELILAH Famous for having cut Samson's hair, she's the perfect short-haired complement for your long-haired SAMSON.

DESDEMONA The heroine of William Shakespeare's tragedy *Othello*, whose love, like your puppy's, never faltered.

DICKENS If barks paid as much as words, this puppy, named after English author Charles Dickens (1812–1870), would be worth a fortune. *See* BOZ.

DIDI Short for DELILAH.

DONNER Don't be surprised if you find this puppy up on the roof sometime.

DOOLITTLE A pup with this name will get along with all the other animals in the household swimmingly well, even the giant pink snails.

DOONESBURY American cartoonist Garry Trudeau created this 1975 Pulitzer Prize–winning comic strip, which satirizes the current political scene. Your puppy, probably much like the Doonesbury characters, will espouse opinions whenever he feels it is necessary.

DOUBLE-O-SEVEN *See* BOND.

DR. WHO This absentminded Galafrayan is the lead character of this BBC television series, the longest-running science fiction show in history. Your equally absentminded, risk-taking puppy, like this character, seems to be blessed with a highly quirky personality.

DRACO An Athenian lawyer who lived circa 621 B.C. and occasionally prescribed the death penalty even for small crimes. His codes are known for harshness in even modern legislation. This puppy doesn't take kindly to forgotten after-dinner treats or playtime.

DROOPY Appropriate name for a Basset Hound or Bloodhound.

DUKE This godfather of soul emanated a quiet resonance, which immediately commanded respect. Maybe your puppy's contemplative, quiet moments are hints to his adult character.

DUNCAN In William Shakespeare's play *Macbeth*, Duncan was the king of Scotland. Now he is the king of your home.

DUN *See* BRADSTREET.

DYLAN Resembling his singer protégé, this pup seems to have a social message set to his own music.

E.T. Extra-terrific puppy!

EINSTEIN The law of gravity is relatively unknown to your jumping creature.

ELMER This puppy may never stop chasing rabbits—even in his sleep.

ELMO Originally Greek, this name meant "amiable," but now widely known as the fuzzy, blue Sesame Street character. It would suit a blue Great Dane, Kerry Blue Terrier, Neapolitan Mastiff or blue Chow Chow.

ELSA From the book and film *Born Free*. This lioness was set free after being raised, rehabilitated and taught how to survive on her own. Your puppy Elsa will never want to leave home.

ELVIRA A mistress of the dark. *See* Coon *in Chapter 2.*

ELVIS Definitely a hound dog who cries all the time.

EMERSON Ralph Waldo Emerson (1803–1882) was an American poet. A puppy named for him will be extremely influential in his own household.

EPSTEIN *See* Sweathog.

EUROPA A Phoenician princess carried by Zeus in the form of a white bull, maybe resembling a Bulldog or Bull Terrier.

EWOK The tribal name for the feisty, warlike characters that appeared in the *Star Wars* saga. Good name for your tough, little terrier puppy.

FATS American singer Fats Domino mixed blues with rock and is best known for his song "Blueberry Hill" (1956). A puppy with this name will give you thrill after thrill.

FAUST A dog with this name thinks he knows everything. Be careful not to make any deals with him. A treat for a trick might not work because, like the magician and alchemist in German legend who sold his soul to the devil in exchange for power and worldly experience, a pup with this name will avoid paying up.

FELIX A puppy with a feline identity crisis who will spend most of his time pawing away at your couch.

FERDINAND The king of Castile from 1474 to 1504. His queen was Isabella. The good home you provide is a castle to your appreciative puppy.

FINN This puppy might be hard to keep in obedience school.

FLETCH A puppy with this name will be humorously devious, like his namesake in this Chevy Chase movie.

FLIPPER Resembling the star dolphin of this television series, a water-loving Labrador Retriever or Portuguese Water Dog will suit this name.

FLOYD Derived from the rock-and-roll group Pink Floyd, or Pretty Boy Floyd, the infamous bank robber. The choice is yours.

FONZI The name of a character in the TV sitcom "Happy Days." This cool puppy really has a heart of gold behind his air of bravado.

FRANKENSTEIN Good name for a Chinese Shar-Pei, Bulldog or Mastiff, or, for fun, a really pretty puppy like an Afghan or Irish Setter.

FRAZIER The psychiatrist from the television series "Cheers." A pup with this name will love hanging out in bars while overanalyzing his friends.

FREUD It seems this puppy's id has taken over.

FRIAR TUCK Appropriate name for a rollicking, pudgy puppy with a zest for adventure.

FRIDAY The humble and devoted companion of Robinson Crusoe, from Daniel Defoe's story *Robinson Crusoe*. This name is perfect for a rescue puppy who will be eternally grateful to you for giving him his life back.

FRITZ Appropriate and popular name for a Dachshund.

FROSTY A white-coated puppy with an aversion to direct sunlight and too much warmth.

FUDD *See* ELMER.

GALILEO Name your puppy for this sixteenth-century Italian scientist and he will always retain a sense of direction and history.

GANDHI Mahatma Gandhi (1869–1948) was an Indian political and spiritual leader who is supposed by many to be the father of independent India. A stubborn puppy can almost rival his namesake's independence.

GARBO Inspired by the famous Swedish actress Greta Garbo, this name confers grace, poise and unmistakable style on your pampered pooch.

GARP The world according to this puppy will be full of treats, playtime and affection.

GATSBY Derived from F. Scott Fitzgerald's protagonist in *The Great Gatsby*, this dog should be forever well groomed, well socialized, and a bit eccentric. His life will be devoted to pleasing the one he loves, you.

GENGHIS Genghis Khan (1162–1227), a Mongolian conqueror who was thought to be a brilliant military strategist. A puppy with this name will be able to plot elaborate schemes to get longer walks at night and more table treats.

GENIE If you pet this puppy enough, your wishes might come true.

GEPPETTO This is the name of the old puppet maker who created Pinocchio. A puppy with this name will know what strings to pull to get what he wants.

GERONIMO For the puppy who will leap head-on into any adventure.

GIDGET A beach puppy who can't stay away from the sand and surf. If you give this little girl a Boogie board she will be quite happy, whether she rides or chews it.

GIGI Good name for a Poodle.

GILLIGAN No matter how good this puppy's intentions are, he will always seem to foul things up.

GODFATHER This puppy will make you an offer you can't refuse.

GODZILLA Good name for a Bloodhound, Great Dane or Mastiff whose large, massive body could overtake any house.

GOETHE The genius of Johann Wolfgang von Goethe (1749–1832), German poet, dramatist, novelist and scientist, encompassed most aspects of human discourse and action. His life, much like yours since this puppy arrived, was augmented by the study of plants and animals.

GOLDILOCKS Good name for a buff Cocker Spaniel, yellow Labrador or Golden Retriever.

GOLIATH Good name for any very large dog or, just for fun, any very small one.

GOMER Named after the television character Gomer Pyle. A clumsy puppy with this name will make many bumbling mistakes look humorous.

GORKY Russian writer Maxim Gorky (1868–1936) is considered the father of Soviet literature. Good name for a Borzoi or Siberian Husky.

GRETEL For a puppy who will follow any trail of crumbs.

GREYSTOKE Swinging from trees, eating bananas and cohorting with jungle beasts are favorite pastimes of all wild puppies.

GROUCHO A puppy with this name will definitely find Daddy's cigars.

GROVER Grover Cleveland was the twenty-second and twenty-fourth president of the United States. A puppy with

HARPO

HERCULES

any presidential name will definitely mismanage your home and run you over budget.

GUINEVERE The wife of King Arthur and presumed mistress of Lancelot. A puppy with this name is worth fighting for.

GULLIVER In Jonathan Swift's story *Gulliver's Travels* (1726) this Englishman travels to the imaginary lands of Lilliput, Brobdingnab, Laputa and Houyhnhnmland. Your puppy might also live in an imaginary land, known as "This House Is My Playpen."

GUMBY The contortionist positions this puppy can twist into are amazing.

HAMLET "A beast that wants discourse of reason," from Act 1, Scene 2, line 150, of William Shakespeare's *Hamlet* (1600–1601). Does your puppy use his sophisticated debate skills on you when he wants something? Those eyes will work every time.

HAMMER For a hyper puppy who looks as if he might dislocate something when he plays.

HANCOCK This puppy will leave his signature everywhere.

HANSEL The opera *Hansel and Gretel* by German composer and teacher Engelbert Humperdinck (1854–1921) is a folk-based fairy tale. *See* GRETEL.

HARPO A comedian by nature, this puppy will know how to get your funny bone.

HARVEY The play and movie *Harvey*, starring Jimmy Stewart, featured an invisible rabbit with this name. This name is appropriate for puppies who hop around like little bunnies, or for puppies who can never be found when you want them. They seem to become invisible.

HAWKEYE A main character on the hit television series "M.A.S.H.," whose sense of humor and practical jokes uplifted the morale of all present, much like your puppy's antics.

HEATHCLIFF A lead character in Emily Brontë's novel *Wuthering Heights*. A puppy with this name will have an almost demonic love for you.

HEIDI This folktale, written by Johanna Spyri in 1881, is set in the Swiss Alps. Good name for a Bernese Mountain Dog or Saint Bernard.

HERCULES A known powerhouse; however, a good name for puppies too small to fit the billing.

HERMES A messenger of the gods, also a god of travelers, luck, music, eloquence, commerce, young men, cheats and thieves. The latter might pertain to your puppy, the shoe thief.

HOBBIT Derived from J.R.R. Tolkien's novel *The Hobbit* (1937). Your fantastical puppy will turn your home into a private kingdom filled with smiles for those he loves.

HOMER A principal figure of ancient Greek literature and the first European poet. Your Homeric puppy must be heroic in proportion, degree and character to deserve this name.

HOMEY The clown ... of your household.

HOOCH The Dogue de Bordeaux in the motion picture *Turner and Hooch* is the inspiration for this name.

HOOK From J. M. Barrie's *Peter Pan*, this dynamic villain insisted on having things his way. Much like a tyrannical puppy, you know?

HOOVER Named after either former President Herbert Hoover, former F.B.I. Director J. Edgar Hoover, or the popular vacuum cleaner company. Hence, this dog is prone to sucking up just about anything.

HORSHACK This funny Sᴡᴇᴀᴛʜᴏɢ from the television show "Welcome Back, Kotter" had a raucous, attention-drawing laugh. Does this resemble your little sweathog's bark?

HORUS In ancient Egyptian religion, he was the sky god of light and goodness. All puppies are inherently filled with goodness, hence this is a good name for any male puppy.

HOUDINI An escape artist. No fence or kennel is too much for this canine magician whose antics will seem to defy explanation.

HUBBLE Robert Redford's character in the movie *The Way We Were*. Good name for a Siberian Husky.

HUCK *See* Fɪɴɴ.

HULK A massive, strong puppy who seems to think butting his head into a wall or door will move it.

HYDE *See* Jekyll.

ICARUS Greek mythology has it that Icarus escaped from Crete on artificial wings made by his father, Daedalus. But in fleeing he flew so close to the sun that the wax that held his wings melted and he fell into the Aegean Sea. For the puppy who jumps from heights as if he thinks he can fly.

IGNATIUS The protagonist of the Pulitzer Prize—winning novel *A Confederacy of Dunces* (1980) by John Kennedy Toole; Ignatius J. Reilly, was a humorous, huge, obese, fastidious Don Quixote of his territory. A puppy with this name will need to have his food intake limited, but definitely not his freedom within your home.

IGOR Named after an infamous butler. The cat in your household will easily point a paw to exclaim that this butler did it.

INDIE Harrison Ford's nickname in the *Indiana Jones* movie series. Good name for a fearless, adventuresome puppy.

ISHTAR The Babylonian goddess of love, fertility and war.

ISIS The Egyptian goddess of fertility.

J.F.K. Ask not what your dog can do for you, but what you can do for your dog.

JAMES DEAN A puppy with this name will become a legend in his own time.

JEDI Short with big ears characterizes a puppy bearing this name.

JEKYLL *The Strange Case of Dr. Jekyll and Mr. Hyde,* by Robert L. Stevenson, presents this character with quasi-schizophrenic alternating phases of kindness and un-kindness, like your puppy when he does or doesn't get enough exercise.

JEMIMA *See* Maple Syrup *in Chapter 2.*

JETHRO The name of the hillbilly nephew on the television show "Beverly Hillbillies." A puppy with this name is endearing though somewhat slow on the uptake.

JUGHEAD Archie's bumbling comic strip friend has now become yours. *See* Archie.

JULIET From Shakespeare's tragedy *Romeo and Juliet.* A puppy with this name will love you devotedly forever.

KAFKA Franz Kafka (1883–1924). *See* Nietzsche.

KANDINSKY Russian artist Wassily Kandinsky (1866–1944) is known primarily for his abstractionist work. Good name for a brightly colored puppy who is easy to spot.

KERMIT *See* Froggy *in Chapter 2.*

KING KONG Named after a misunderstood giant go-rilla, this puppy will go to all lengths to prove his devotion. He is truly an interesting specimen. Good name for a strangely proportioned and oversized mixed-breed dog.

J.F.K.

KOSMO

KIPLING English author Rudyard Kipling (1865–1936) is most notably known for his work interpreting India and its strife, as well as for winning the 1907 Nobel Prize in literature; however, you and your puppy can probably more closely identify with his children's story *The Jungle Book*.

KOKO This is the name of an intelligent gorilla who effectively learned sign language. Your pup should show signs of unusual learning ability to be given this name.

KOSMO A good Gremlin. Suits a French Bulldog or Pekingese.

KUJO Although this puppy may seem to have multiple personalities, it is probably just his way of telling you that he wants multiple toys.

LADY This flirtatious Cocker Spaniel was the object of Tramp's affection in the Disney movie *Lady and the Tramp*.

LANCELOT A knight of the Round Table whose love affair with Queen Guinevere resulted in a war with King Arthur. A puppy with this name will go to all lengths to win your love.

LASSIE In 1941 a Collie named Pal passed a screen test and became the world-renowned Lassie. Pal was purchased for five dollars and was chosen over three hundred other dogs for the part. Definitely an old classic name for a Collie.

LAZARUS This character returned from the dead. Good name for a rescue puppy.

LILITH A psychiatrist's wife in the hit television series "Cheers." A puppy with this name is thin, sexy and outspoken.

LINUS Puppies get attached to their blankets and leashes also.

LIONHEART King Richard I, otherwise known as "Coeur de Lion" or "the Lion-Hearted," ruled from 1157 to 1199. He became a romantic figure in England due to his military prowess there. Good name for a Mastiff or Rhodesian Ridgeback.

LOBO Your Alaskan Malamute might resemble this famous wolf.

LOLITA Modeled after author Vladimir Nabokov's title character in his novel *Lolita*, this puppy will probably look and act older than she really is.

LOVEY This puppy was practically shipwrecked on an island of loneliness before she met you.

LUDWIG If you like Beethoven, let your Doberman tell the world.

MACBETH The protagonist of Shakespeare's tragedy *Macbeth* has been described as overimaginative and prone to visions. Behavior such as this can make raising your little monster difficult, but worthwhile.

MACHIAVELLI Suggestive of or characterized by principles of expediency and cunning, like a puppy who becomes angry with his people for leaving him alone too long.

MAD MAX A bit crazy, but able to overcome most any obstacle is how this valorous puppy lives life.

MADAME BUTTERFLY This opera (1904) by Italian composer Giacomo Puccini is extremely sentimental in nature, much like your loving, emotional puppy.

MAGGIE This puppy probably walks as gingerly as a cat on a hot tin roof.

MANCHU One of the nomadic Mongoloid people native to Manchuria who conquered China in 1644 and established a dynasty, which was overthrown in 1911. Good name for a dog whose ancestry traces to China; Pekingese and Shih Tzus apply.

MARIE ANTOINETTE (1755–1793) The queen of France who was executed due to what some deemed treasonous behavior—but what style!

MARILYN Marilyn Monroe (1926–1962). For a precious femme fatale puppy who will need a lot of love and at rare intervals may exhibit signs of having real talent. This puppy also has to be a blonde.

MARLEY The ghost of Ebenezer Scrooge's partner in Charles Dickens's *A Christmas Carol*. The ghost showed Scrooge the beauty of life, as this giving puppy will do for you. This name also refers to the reggae singer Bob Marley, known for his dreadlocks, much like a Komondor or Puli.

MARMADUKE Brad Anderson created this comic strip adult Great Dane with constant puppy behavior in 1924.

MATISSE French painter, sculptor and lithographer Henri Matisse (1869–1954) painted an impressionist work that might be of particular interest to your puppy: "The Dinner Table" (1897). This was also the name of the Border Collie who starred in the feature film *Down and Out in Beverly Hills*.

MAYA In Roman mythology she was the goddess of earth and growth. Good name for a puppy destined to grow considerably.

MEDEA This Greek mythological figure is famed for her skill in sorcery, especially fire creation. Good name for a fiery-tempered dog.

MEDUSA In Greek mythology, one of the three Gorgons who had serpents for hair, bronze claws and huge teeth.

MERLIN A magician of a puppy who will turn the neatest of homes and wardrobes into a shambles.

MICKEY Good name for a miniature, mouse-sized male puppy.

MIDAS In Greek mythology this king was given the power to turn everything he touched into gold, but when his food became gold he decided to rid himself of his power. It is rare for a puppy to increase the material value of anything in your home, but one with a name like this has the best chance.

MINERVA The goddess of wisdom, invention, the arts and martial prowess in Roman mythology. A puppy with this name has some big paws to fill.

MINNIE Good name for a tiny, mouse-sized female doggie.

MIRÓ Joan Miró (1893–1983) used images from the subconscious as the basis for his surreal work. This could be your puppy's inspiration also.

MISHA An affectionate pet name for both the Soviet dancer Mikhail Baryshnikov and your graceful puppy.

MO-JO A nickname for the rock-and-roll singer Jim Morrison from the group "The Doors." A puppy with this name might be a bit rebellious and confused, but he is really a poet at heart.

MONA LISA For a puppy with a timeless face and smile.

MORK Like this alien character from the television show "Mork & Mindy" your puppy may seem to come from another planet.

MORTIMER This recurring name in Shakespeare's historical plays usually connotes an earl or other nobleman; therefore it is suitable for your royal puppy.

MOZART A prodigy pup with an ear for music.

MUDD Physician Samuel Mudd (1833–1883) treated John Wilkes Booth's broken leg and was later convicted for conspiring in the assassination plot against Abraham Lincoln. This name is also appropriately funny for a puppy who simply loves to play in the mud and occasionally leaves telling tracks across the floor, sofa or bed.

MUGSY *See* BUGSY.

MUMBLES It is hard to make sense of this puppy's whines.

MUSE In Greek mythology, any of the nine daughters of Mnemosyne and Zeus, each of whom presided over a different art or science. Also a guiding spirit or source of inspiration, much like your puppy's undying affection for you.

NAPOLEON English author Aldous Huxley wrote, "To his dog, every man is Napoleon; hence the popularity of dog." Of course the inverse of this statement is true, hence the popularity of this name. Good name for your overly territorial pooch.

NEWTON Sir Isaac Newton (1642–1727) was an English mathematician, scientist and philosopher. A puppy with this name will breeze through his schooling.

NICKLEBY In the Dickens novel *Nicholas Nickleby* (1839) the protagonist suffered many cruelties before rising above his circumstances. This name would surely suit a rescue puppy.

NIETZSCHE Friedrich Wilhelm Nietzsche (1844–1900) was a leader of existential doctrine and literature. With this name, your dog might at times seem a bit detached. Just give him a toy and some love and he will be all right.

NOEL A Christmas puppy, who mirrors the joy of the festive season throughout the year.

O.J. Named after the athlete O. J. Simpson, therefore appropriate for a puppy with elusive speed; or an acronym for orange juice, because, like your vitamin C fix in the morning, you simply can't live without this puppy.

OBERON In medieval folklore he was King of the Fairies. A puppy with this name will be flighty and tricky, but oh so lovable.

OLD YELLER Obviously a good name for a yellow Labrador.

OPHELIA She was the object of the protagonist's affection in Shakespeare's tragedy *Hamlet*. Now this puppy is the object of yours.

ORION A giant hunter who is killed by Artemis. Good name for any hunting dog. *See* Birdy *in Chapter 2*.

ORPHAN ANNIE Definitely a redhead who you probably adopted from the local shelter. *See* Red *in Chapter 2*.

OTHELLO In this Shakespearean play this lead character presents the audience with conflicting forces of order and chaos, good and evil. Does this remind you of a puppy who has and has not had enough exercise?

OZZIE Good name for an Australian Shepherd or Terrier.

PADDINGTON *See* Bear *in Chapter 2*.

PARIS In Greek mythology he was the Prince of Troy whose abduction of Helen provoked the Trojan War. A puppy with this name may incite small feuds at the park by taking other puppies' toys.

PATTON General George Smith Patton is known for his hot temper, much like a little puppy when he doesn't get to sleep on the bed.

PAVLOV This puppy may need a bib for his drooling.

PEASEBLOSSOM A fairy in Shakespeare's play *A Midsummer Night's Dream*. *See* Oberon.

PEBBLES This puppy takes its name from a character in "The Flintstones."

PENELOPE In Greek mythology she was the wife of Odysseus and a model of fidelity. A puppy with this name will never leave your side.

PERITAR Alexander the Great founded a city of this name after this courageous dog who fought a lion.

PERSEUS The son of Zeus and Danae in Greek mythology who slew Medusa and rescued Andromeda. You and your house are safe with this fearless puppy around.

PETRARCH This Italian poet inspired the creation of the sonnet. Good name for an Italian Greyhound or Maltese.

PICASSO Pablo Picasso (1881–1973). A Spanish artist who worked in both France and Spain and is known primarily for his cubism and abstractionism. Your pup might tend to model his style with his abstract home "redecorating" ability. Picasso's pets were a goat and Boxer.

PICKWICK This series of Charles Dickens's sketches, *The Pickwick Papers*, is famous for its humor. Your new puppy will bring as many smiles into your home.

PINOCCHIO Originally an Italian character from a story created by Carlo Collodi in 1892. Good name for a puppy with a long muzzle that grows longer with every devious puppy act: Borzoi, Doberman Pinscher, Saluki.

PIPPI Pippi Longstocking, a mischievous storybook girl who is known for her valor in saving her friends and father from danger. Cute name for a puppy with similar pigtails. If you say this puppy's name fast, it's funny.

PLATO You have an extremely moral and righteous pup on your hands who probably "spouts off" a little more than you can digest.

PLUTO Typified in cartoons as a bumbling hound.

POINDEXTER A puppy with a high I.Q. deserves this name. Obedience school will be a cinch for this brainy puppy.

POLLY Polly wanna treat?

POOH Winnie-the-Pooh was created by A. A. Milne in 1927. *See* BEAR *in Chapter 2.*

POPEYE A little spinach on puppy's kibble never hurt.

PORTIA The wife of BRUTUS in Shakespeare's play *Julius Caesar*. These are good companion names for a two-dog household.

PRANCER Good name for an Afghan Hound, or any dog who moves with the grace of a flying reindeer.

PRUDENCE This little dear of a puppy will not be hard to convince to come out and play.

PUCK A mischievous fairy from Shakespeare's play *A Midsummer Night's Dream*, who will probably create as much chaos in your home as he did in his forest.

PUFF Your puppy, like this magical dragon, will anxiously await your every return in order to frolic gleefully with you, in the autumn mist or anytime.

PUNCH This puppy knows what strings to pull to get what he or she wants.

QUASIMODO Italian author Salvatore Quasimodo (1901–1968) won the Nobel Prize in 1959. Good name for a Neapolitan Mastiff.

QUIXOTE Derived from Cervantes's fictional character Don Quixote. Daydreamer, courageous, independent, adventurous and troublemaker all describe this puppy.

RAGGEDY ANN There are few things as cuddly and comforting as this puppy. This doll's raggedy hair might also bring to mind your puppy with her similarly tousled locks.

RAMBO A fictional Vietnam hero with superhuman survivalist instincts. This puppy makes coming home a booby-trapped adventure.

RASCAL As in the old television series "The Little Rascals." A puppy bearing this name has a little bit of ALFALFA, BUCKWHEAT and SPANKY all rolled up into one mischievous pooch.

RASSELAS A puppy with this name will definitely be the object of your affection. Named after the moral romance by English author Samuel Johnson (1759).

RAVEL French composer Maurice Joseph Ravel (1875–1937) is known for his orchestral works, especially his 1928 composition *Bolero*. Good name for Ibizan Hound.

RAVEN *See* B*LACKIE* *in Chapter 2.*

REDBEARD Named after this pirate and ghost. *See* R*ED* *in Chapter 2.*

RHETT If you wonder why obedience training is not working, it is because this puppy simply doesn't give a d———.

RICKY-TICKY-TAVI A brave mongoose with this name saved his friend's life by wrestling with a cobra until both died. A puppy with this name will always heroically protect you.

RIN TIN TIN An extremely intelligent German Shepherd Dog who served as a messenger and was wounded in World War I. Within a year after the war he made his way to Hollywood and starred in twenty-two films.

RINGO This star drummer and composer is known for his musical talents. Your puppy may so far be known only for his noisemaking ability.

RIP VAN WINKLE Puppy naps sneak up quickly and can last for quite some time with this one, if you are lucky.

RIPLEY Believe it or not, this puppy is all yours.

ROB ROY A fabled Scottish hero, like your bold Westie pup.

ROCKY A tough fighter. Good name for a Boxer.

ROGAN A sports aficionado's companion.

ROMEO Known as the quintessential male love, just like your male puppy. They should all be so cavalier.

ROMULUS In Roman mythology he was the son of Mars and the legendary founder of Rome. Good name for a territorial puppy who will insist on "marking" his territory.

RUMPELSTILTSKIN A German fairy tale by the brothers Grimm in which a man spun straw into gold in exchange for the miller's daughter. If possible, your inspired puppy would undoubtedly perform this task for you.

SAM-I-AM For the puppy who will eat just about anywhere: in a house, with a mouse, in a train, even in the rain.

SAMMY A popular pet name for dogs of both sexes in wide use everywhere.

SAMSON A judge of Israel of extraordinary physical strength. His strength was said to be found in his long hair. Good name for a Komondor, Old English Sheepdog or Puli; just don't have him trimmed too short.

SANTINI See HOUDINI.

SATCHMO See ARMSTRONG.

SCARLET A name popularized by the heroine of the novel *Gone with the Wind* by Margaret Mitchell in 1936. The character's full name was Katie Scarlet O'Hara. This name is of Middle English derivation meaning "deep red color." *See* Red *in Chapter 2.*

SCHWARZKOPF A tactical, calculating puppy who will run a tight household or force you to do so.

SCOOBIE Good name for a Great Dane, who loves snacks.

SCRAPPY TOO *See* Scoobie.

SCROOGE Ebenezer Scrooge was a miserly character who eventually saw the light in *A Christmas Carol* by Charles Dickens (1812–1870). A puppy with this name will inevitably learn that the rewards for good behavior outweigh those for bad.

SCYLLA In Greek mythology she was a female sea monster who devoured sailors. A cute name for a harmless-looking puppy.

SHAKESPEARE "For thy part, I do wish thou wert a dog, / That I might love thee something." (*Timon of Athens*, Act 4, Scene 3)

SHAMU Named after a famous killer whale housed in Sea World. This puppy promises to grow to equal proportions if he keeps receiving too many table scraps.

SHELLEY Good name for a Shetland Sheepdog because these dogs are affectionately known as Shelties.

SHERLOCK Sherlock Holmes, famous detective of fiction, was introduced in 1887 by his creator, Sir Arthur Conan

Doyle. If yours is an especially inquisitive puppy, this name is ideal. *See* BEARLOCK HOLMES *in Chapter 2.*

SHIVA In Hinduism she is the god of destruction and reproduction, and is a member of a Hindu triad. A flirtatious puppy who will normally leave your house in shambles deserves this name.

SHYLOCK A usurer from Shakespeare's *The Merchant of Venice*. This puppy accepts treats, toys or affection as a form of repayment for good behavior.

SILVER The Lone Ranger's trusty white horse, or your faithful Greyhound, Weimaraner or Kerry Blue.

SIMPLY RED *See* RED *in Chapter 2.*

SINATRA Unlike his mentor, it is doubtful that this puppy's "singing" will sway you into a mellow mood.

SINBAD This is a character in one of a series of stories in *A Thousand and One Nights* or *Arabian Nights* in which the hero battles for his life. A puppy with this name will more than likely grow up to be a relentlessly courageous dog.

SITTING BULL When gold was found in the Black Hills, Sitting Bull led the Sioux resistance against the prospectors. A pup with this name will defiantly stand up for his tennis balls and Frisbees. Good name for a Bulldog, Bullmastiff or Bull Terrier.

SKYWALKER The force is with this puppy.

SLEESTACK These evil creatures from the 1970s cartoon "Land of the Lost" had strange snouts and irregular breathing, like some long-nosed Doberman Pinschers.

SITTING BULL

SNEEZY For a puppy whose actions fit the name.

SNOOPY Definitely a Beagle.

SOCRATES Good name for a puppy who intuitively figures things out: how to open doors, climb fences, get into the fridge . . . Pretty soon he will be driving himself to the park. Hide the car keys!

SOLOMON This puppy will develop a natural wisdom.

SPANKY This cherubic little puppy will occasionally get caught in compromising situations but is smart about getting out of them.

SPOCK Perfect for a dog with long, pointed ears. Possibly a name for a Chihuahua, Chinese Crested or Xoloitzcuintli.

SPUDS Good name for a Bull Terrier.

STING This musically inclined puppy will be a legend in his own time.

SEUSS Theodore Seuss Geisel (1904–1991), also known as Dr. Seuss, created whimsical, crazy, outlandish children's books that your puppy would love to have read to him as bedtime stories.

SUNDANCE *See* Butch, Cassidy.

SWEATHOG Obedience school will probably be difficult for a misfit puppy with this name. Just make sure you give him all the help he needs. *See* Barbarino.

TARZAN Edgar Rice Burroughs, American novelist, created this character in his 1914 story *Tarzan of the Apes*. The outdoor life is definitely suitable to this bohemian, ill-mannered puppy who will turn your house into a jungle.

TAUSKEY Rudolph William Tauskey died in 1979 at the age of ninety-one. He was the only official photographer ever retained by the American Kennel Club, 1924–1942. A puppy with this name should be immortalized in pictures, if only in your photo album.

TERMINATOR A puppy so well built that you'd think he was a machine.

THATCHER Good name for a female Bulldog.

THUMPER *See* BUNNY *in Chapter 2.*

TIGGER Your puppy, named for Winnie the Pooh's trusty friend, will serve you just as well.

TINKERBELL A puppy with this name will bounce around the house like a fiery ball of light and will take you to the magical limits of the universe.

TINMAN Unlike the character he imitates, it is doubtful that this puppy lacks a heart.

TOMBA A four-time Olympic downhill skiing medalist who stole the hearts of his Italian homeland as well as the entire female population. Your athletic, flamboyant puppy with this name will do the same.

TONTO A puppy with this name is destined to be a trusty companion. Appropriate name for puppies who promise to grow to horse size.

TOTO Say "Toto" and most people see a Cairn Terrier! In L. Frank Baum's book *Wonderful Wizard of Oz* (1900), Toto was the pivotol character, and was portrayed by a Cairn in the classic movie version.

TRAMP Always ready and willing to give affection, especially to his lady.

TRUFFAUT Here is a name for a puppy who should be in pictures. François Truffaut (1932–1984) was a French film director who created films with strong visual effect—just like your puppy.

TRUMP For a puppy who likes to have things his way.

TUTU Desmond Mpilo Tutu is a South African religious leader who won the 1984 Nobel Peace Prize. A puppy with this name is unquestionably a leader who has no fear of blazing new trails to human understanding.

TWEETY For a puppy with an identity crisis. This little puppy, oddly enough, will always run from the cat.

ULYSSES A Greek commander, who now runs your home.

UMPA LUMPA In the movie and book *Willy Wonka and the Chocolate Factory* by Roald Dahl, the umpa lumpas were hardworking, loyal midgets, much like your miniature puppy.

VAN GOGH This puppy's art might be better appreciated later in life.

VAN-DAMME A puppy with all the right moves.

VENUS DE MILO Needless to say, this puppy stole your heart at first glance.

VENUS The Roman goddess of natural productivity, love and beauty. A name such as this pays homage to the equivalent beauty of your pooch.

VOLTAIRE François Marie Arouet Voltaire (1694–1778) was a French philosopher, author and editor of the first French encyclopedia. An intelligent and creative pup, French or not, deserves this name.

WARHOL Your puppy's pop icon "decorations" around the house can sometimes be interpreted as art, even those cans he drags out of the garbage.

WILBUR This is the name of the pig in *Charlotte's Web*. If it suits your puppy, it can also be his. *See* CHARLOTTE *in this chapter and* PIGGY *in Chapter 1.*

WILSON Woodrow Wilson, twenty-eighth United States president. *See* GROVER.

WINSTON See CHURCHILL.

WOODY Like his protégé Woody the Woodpecker, a puppy with this name will make lasting, indelible marks on your heart and furniture.

WOOKIE A large furry humanoid from the movie *Star Wars. See* SASQUATCH *in Chapter 2.*

WRIGLEY William Wrigley, Jr., an American chewing gum manufacturer, and the name of Wrigley Field, home field of the Chicago Cubs. Good name for a baseball aficionado's companion.

WUNDERDOG A superhuman, law-abiding Beagle.

YEAGER Chuck Yeager. The first aviator pilot to fly at the speed of sound. A quintessential American hero. A fearless pup who may break the speed of sound when he hears dinner is being served can proudly bear this name.

YODA *See* JEDI.

YOGI BEAR No campsite is secure with this curious puppy rummaging about.

ZEPPELIN *See* FLOYD.

ZEPPO Good name for the third pup if the other two are named GROUCHO and HARPO. See either.

ZIGGY A cherubic cartoon character or your equally portly and comical pup.

ZOPPICO The Greek author Plutarch told a story about this Poodle-like dog who performed for an emperor two thousand years ago. The story demonstrated the dog's desire to be a ham in front of others. Maybe your pup has this same desire.

ZORRO *The Mark of Zorro* (1920) starring Douglas Fairbanks is a classic swashbuckler film. Does the name work for your swashbuckler puppy?

ZSA ZSA Good name for a lap dog with a bit of an attitude.

ZEUS The father and ruler of all gods now oversees your home. Good for pooches who will probably develop strong, protective tendencies.

4

Back to Basics

ANY LUCKY PUPPIES are given human names, such as Humphrey, Max or Lucy. This is a wonderful way to include your puppy as a family member; however, unless the chosen name has been passed down from generation to generation its origin has probably been lost. This chapter is designed for pet owners who like the idea of a traditional puppy/human name but would like to know its meaning and origin.

ABBY A short form of Abigail. This name in Latin or Hebrew is translated to mean "father's joy."

ABEL The name means "meadow" and signifies fruitfulness. In Hebrew it translates to mean "breath."

ALASTAIR This name is a form of Alexander. From Greek meaning "the vindicator."

ALDO Of German translation meaning "old."

ALGER Derived from Anglo-Saxon translation meaning "warrior" or "noble spearman."

ARI This name signifies power and in Hebrew translates to mean "lion."

ARTY A common form of Arthur. This name signifies height and strength. From Gaelic meaning "noble, hill or bear."

AUSTIN A variant form for August. From Latin translation meaning "exalted, revered." *See* Augustus *in Chapter 3.*

BABBIT Old English nickname for "babe" or "infant."

BABETTE A shorter form of Barbara. Translated in many European languages to mean "a foreigner."

BALDWIN Known as a very old English name meaning "bold in war" or "bold friend."

BARNEY A variation of Barnaby or Bernard. It means "speech."

BARTON A variation of Bartholomew. The Anglo-Saxon translation is "barley town." It also signifies a guarding quality.

BEN A short version of Benjamin. It means "son" in Hebrew.

BENNINGTON This name originally meant one who came from Bennington, a village of dwellers on the Beane river in England.

BENTLEY A common local name in England originally stemming from the term for a clearing overgrown with bent grass, and those who came from there.

BERTHA From the Old Germanic meaning "intelligent" or "popular."

BESSIE A popular diminutive of Elizabeth, which is of Hebrew derivation, meaning "God's oath."

BIDDY (BRIDGET)—"Strength" in Celtic.

BINA Yiddish for "bee."

BLANCHE Ancient French, Italian and English meaning "pale" or "light in color."

BOB The name of the first Bulldog registered with the AKC, in 1886. This name stems from "Robert," which means "bright and wise."

BORIS "Battling warrior" in Russian.

BRUNHILDA Old Germanic for "beast" or "brown battlemaid."

BRUNO The old German meaning of this word was "brown or dark in appearance."

BUDD A short variation of Baldwin. The Old English meaning is "messenger."

BYRON From the Teutonic meaning "from the cottage."

CALVIN Latin for "bald."

CAROLINA French meaning "strong, virile."

CASEY A Celtic name meaning "valorous or brave," which probably explains why so many dogs of so many breeds are named this.

CASPAR From the Old Germanic meaning "regal" or "imperial."

CASSIE (CASSANDRA)—This name means "one who incites love." In Greek legend she was a prophetess, but her predictions were never believed although many occurred, much like your puppy's reasons for whimpering and whining at times.

CECIL Latin for "poor-sighted" or "blind."

CECILY A feminine variant of Cecil.

CHELSEA Originally a place where chalk and limestone sediment piled up in London. Use of this as a first name is thought to have begun in Australia.

CHESTER Derived from Middle English, this name is said to come from the word for town or city.

CHLOE From late Greek meaning "budding."

CLEMENTINE Latin for "merciful."

CLEO "Of royal descent, distinguished" in Greek.

CLYDE "Quite loud" in Welsh.

CODY This nickname for "Conrad" connotes a wise helper.

CONAN Celtic for "bright" or "chief."

CORY Translated from Old English to mean "a selected person."

CRAWFORD "Craw" stems from an early English pronunciation of the word "crow," and a "ford" is a shallow area of water, hence "Crawford" means a shallow area of water to which crows flock.

CRYSTAL Derived from Greek "krystallos," which means "ice." This name denotes expensive cut glass.

CZAR A king or emperor; a tyrant or autocrat. *See* CAESAR *in Chapter 3.*

DESIREE Latin for "desire" or "desirable."

DOLLY Old English pet name that means "a doll."

DOOGIE A pet form of Douglas meaning "black water" in Gaelic.

DUDLEY A name that originally signified a meadow in Worcester, England.

DUSTY A diminutive of Dustin. Old Germanic for "courageous warrior."

ELIAS A prophet with international stature whose "lord is his god."

ELROY In Latin and French this name loosely translates to mean "imperial, king."

EMILY A medieval name meaning "motivated" and "ambitious."

EMMA Occasionally used as a pet form of EMILY, but originally Old Germanic for "a grand person."

ENZO A popular modern variation of such Italian names as Vincenzo and Lorenzo, which translate to mean "conquerer" and "crowned with laurel," respectively.

ERROL The Latin translation is "roamer."

FRANKIE Other popular variations are Francis or Frank. This is an Old Germanic name meaning "liberal."

GAVIN Arthurian legend christened one of the knights of the Round Table with this name meaning "little hawk" in ancient European translation.

GEORGIA The state of Georgia was named after King George II. It is referred to as the Peach, Goober and Buzzard state. In Greek this name is thought to mean a "husband, woman or farmer."

GERTRUDE Old Dutch, German and possibly English for "a strong warrior."

GIDEON Hebrew for "a powerful fighter."

GISELLE Of French, English and Germanic origin meaning "a promise."

GOLDIE Old German, Hebrew and Yiddish for "golden-haired."

GRACE From Latin meaning the same—"grace."

GUNTHER The protagonist of Wagner's opera *Götterdammerung* (1876), whose tragic life story immortalized this name. The Anglo-Saxon translation is "warrior."

GUS A derivative of August, from Augustus Caesar.

GUSSY A feminine version of Gus.

GUY Loosely translated in French to mean "a leader, or guide."

HASKELL Of medieval derivation, this name means "strong commander."

HERMAN From Old Germanic meaning "fighter."

HILDA *See* Matilda.

HOLLY A plant used in English homes with the hope that it would bring good luck. The Anglo-Saxon meaning of this name is "holy."

HOPE English for "faith."

HORACE Latin for "hour keeper."

HORATIO A derivative of HORACE.

HOWARD Throughout all its confused origins, this name has consistently signified a protector.

HUDSON A derivative of the Hebrew name "Hod." This name means the "son of splendor or vigor."

HUGO From Old Germanic meaning "intelligent leader or warrior."

HUMPHREY A loose Anglo-Saxon translation meaning "securer of the home."

IDA "A happy and hard worker" of varied European derivation.

IRA A name of Hebrew origin having conflicting meaning: "attentiveness" or "ancestry."

ISABELLE Latin for "beautiful honey bee."

JAKE A derivative of the Hebrew name "Jacob," which means "supplanted" or "held by the heel."

JASPER "A bearer of precious gifts or secrets." Probably derived from the name of one of the three wise men.

JED "Hand" in Arabic.

JESSE "Gift" in Hebrew.

JEZEBEL Hebrew meaning "impure."

KAYLE In Hebrew this name signifies idyllic beauty, perfection and glory.

LACEY An Old Irish surname.

LEILA Arabic, Persian and Hebrew meaning "a dark-haired beauty."

LEO A name that signifies strength. "Lion" in Greek, late Latin and English.

LOLA A variant of Dolores, which in Spanish means "sorrows."

LULU This nickname for Louise means a remarkable action or object.

MAC Irish Gaelic for "the son of."

MACMILLAN "A devotee of a particular saint" in Old Scottish.

MALCOLM Latin and Arabic for "dove."

MAMIE Hebrew for "anger and sadness."

MANDY Latin for "to love."

MATILDA "Powerful in battle or a battlemaid" is the derivation of this Old German and Anglo-Saxon name.

MATOK Meaning "sweet" in Hebrew.

MATTIE Short for MATILDA.

MAX This name, currently enjoying enormous popularity, is a contraction of Maximilian.

MAYNARD A Norman and German surname meaning "strong and courageous."

MELVIN Of Celtic origin meaning "commander or leader."

MILES "Adored" in German or "soldier" in Greek and Latin.

MISSIE "Young lady" in contemporary American usage.

MONA Greek for "single or alone."

MONTY In French this name referred to a mountain dweller.

MORRIS Latin for "dark-toned," or Gaelic for "great fighter."

MORTIMER A location name in Old French originally referring to stagnant, still water.

NELLIE Old European for "faint coloring."

NIKITA Translated in some European languages to mean "small victory."

NIKO Masculine version of NIKITA.

NINA "Young girl" in Spanish. Also, possibly of Babylonian origin meaning "granddaughter."

NISSAN Originally Hebrew meaning "escape."

NOAH Of Hebrew origin meaning "to comfort."

OKIE A diminutive for Okon meaning "born at night" in Nigerian.

OLIVER Much like "an olive tree," this name symbolizes peace.

OLLIE A variant of OLIVER.

OMAR A name of Arabic origin meaning "first son."

OSCAR A name of Old European origin meaning "jumping soldier."

OTIS Of Greek origin meaning "good hearing."

OTTO Old English or German meaning "wealthy."

OZ A variant of Oswald. Hebrew for "a ruler of the house." This name signifies a helper.

PACO A Spanish variant of FRANKIE.

PALOMA This name signifies "dove" in Spanish.

PEABODY This Old English word could have originally been a name for a "showy" person.

PEPE Short for Franciscito, the Spanish version of FRANKIE.

PERSEPHONE In Greek mythology, she was the wife of Pluto and queen of the Underworld. What's a nice puppy like yours doing with a job like that?

PETULIA This name originated from Late Latin word "petulare" and means "to ask." It can also be associated with the flower petunia.

QUINCY A Latin surname meaning "the fifth son's estate," probably derived from the family that owned property at Cuinchy in Normandy.

RALPH Old English or Germanic for "wolf-counsel."

RAY From Old French and Spanish meaning "king."

REMINGTON In Old English this was a stream in Yorkshire, England. Hence, this name was given as a surname to the dwellers who settled near this stream.

REMY Short for REMINGTON.

REX Latin for "king."

RHEA Greek for "poppy." Also one of several flightless, three-toed birds of the genus *Rhea*.

ROSCOE Old English for "graceful hoofstock."

ROTHSCHILD This was both an Ashkenazic and British surname derived from a house of the same name, which was distinguished by a red shield.

ROXANNE Originally of Persian origin, but also Old European for "dawn."

ROXY Short for ROXANNE.

RUPERT A variant of Robert. *See* BOB.

SABBATH Short for Elizabeth. *See* BESSIE.

SADIE "Princess" in Hebrew.

SALVATORE Of Latin origin meaning "to save."

SAM Of Hebrew origin meaning "he is God" or a "prophet or judge."

SANTO Of Spanish origin for "saint."

SASHA An English derivation of the Soviet nickname for Alexandra.

SAVANNAH "A great treeless plain" in Anglo-Saxon.

SEYMOUR From Old Germanic meaning "famed at sea" or Teutonic meaning "sower."

SHANE Yiddish for "beautiful."

SHEBA The name originates from Saba, an ancient country once part of Saudi Arabia.

SIDNEY It is believed that this name is from a Phoenician root meaning "charmer" or "captivating."

SIEGFRIED Old Germanic for "victory" and "peace."

SIGMUND Old Germanic for "victory" and "protector."

SINCLAIR A name originating from a French family whose manor on the property was titled Saint-Sinclair.

SOPHIE Of Greek origin meaning "wisdom."

STELLA "Star" in Latin.

TAMARA Of Hebrew origin meaning "palm," or also East Indian for "spice."

TARA Of Gaelic origin meaning "hill."

TESS Short for Theresa, which in Greek means "cultivator."

THOR Old Germanic for "thunder."

THURMAN Old Germanic for "having orange, shaggy hair."

TILLY See MATILDA.

TOBY The feminine form of Tobias. Hebrew for "good."

VALENTINO Of Latin origin meaning "strong and healthy."

WALDO Old English for "powerful" and "distinguished."

WANDA From the Old Germanic meaning "roamer."

WILFRED From the Old Germanic meaning "peacefulness" or "complacency."

WILHELMINA A feminine variant of William meaning "desire" and "protection." The name was introduced to England by the Normans.

WILLOUGHBY An English location name derived from a settlement near the willows.

WINDSOR Derived from a place "near the river's bend" near Berkshire, England.

WINTHROP Now an American name, this name originated in England and signifies a friendly village.

WOLFGANG An Old Germanic common name meaning "where the wolf goes."

ZEKE Of possible Arabic origin meaning "a comet or shooting star."

ZELDA A common German name meaning "happiness" or "good fortune."

ZELIG A popular Yiddish name meaning "a gifted spirit."

ZOE "Life."

FRED & GINGER

SAKE & SUSHI

5

Good Things Come in Twos

Having more than one canine inhabiting your home can be chaotic enough without the added possibility of an identity crisis. If you have more than one dog you can avoid confusion by making sure their names sound different. The names not only should *be* different, but should also *sound* different to the dogs. "Huey and Louie" and "Hekyll and Jekyll" may be distinguishable to you, but for puppies who can hardly discern right from wrong, the ability to recognize a consonant's difference is a stretch. Both puppies will forever respond when only one is called.

If you already have a dog, the introduction of a new one can prove to be problematic enough without the added confusion of similar names. The elder dog will adapt more quickly to the newcomer if you give them distinct identities. The puppy's name again should sound completely different. The older dog will not take kindly to an impertinent little puppy who always responds when he or she is actually the one being called. The older dogs's space and home will be

239

further invaded. Ultimately, the puppy will have a harder time learning his or her name if he or she is forever responding to commands given to the older dog and finding a frustrated owner instead of a reward. If your dogs' names simply must complement each other try something like "Wolfgang and Puck" or "Lady and Tramp."

ABBOTT & COSTELLO
ABERCROMBIE & FITCH
ABOVE & BEYOND
ALPHA & BETA
ANTONY & CLEOPATRA
ASSET & LIABILITY
BALL & CHAIN
BACON & TOMATO
BAMBI & FLOWER
BAREFOOT &
   CONTESSA
BAUSCH & LOMB
BEAUTY & BEAST
BELUGA & CAVIAR
BEN & JERRY
BENSON & HEDGES
BENTLEY & ROLLS
BLACK & BLUE
BOLD & BEAUTIFUL
BONNIE & CLYDE
BUMP & GRIND
BUTTONS & BOWS
CALVIN & HOBBES
CHILI & PEPPER
CAUSE & EFFECT
CEASE & DESIST

CHARLOTTE, EMILY &
   ANNE
CHILE & RELLENO(S)
CHOCOLATE & CHIP(S)
CHOCOLATE &
   VANILLA
COOKIE(S) & CREAM
COP(S) & ROBBER(S)
COUSTEAU & CALYPSO
COWBOY(S) &
   INDIAN(S)
CRIME(S) &
   MISDEMEANOR(S)
CRIMSON & CLOVER
CRUSADER & MOORE
CRUSOE & FRIDAY
DANNY & LIBBY
DAZED & CONFUSED
(TWEEDLE)DEE &
   (TWEEDLE)DUM
DIAMOND(S) &
   PEARL(S)
DONNER & BLITZEN
DUN & BRADSTREET
EBONY & IVORY
EDITH & ARCHIE

EGG & DROP
ERNIE & BERT
FELIX & OSCAR
FINDER(S) &
   KEEPER(S)
FIRE & ICE
FIRE & RAIN
FLORA & FAUNA
FORTNUM & MASON
FRANKIE & JOHNNIE
FRAZIER & LILITH
FRED & GINGER
FRUSEN & GLADJE
GEPPETTO &
   PINOCCHIO
GIN & TONIC
GRIN & BEAR IT
GROUCHO, HARPO &
   ZEPPO
GUMBY & POKEY
GUNS & ROSES
HAM & EGGS
HEART & SOUL
HEALTHCLIFF &
   CATHERINE
HERE & NOW
HOPE(S) & DREAM(S)
IGGY & POP
JEFF & RADAR
JEKYLL & HYDE
JET & SHARK
JUGHEAD & ARCHIE
KAHLUA & CREAM
KIBBLES & BITS

KISS & TELL
KIT & CABOODLE
LAUREL & HARDY
LEATHER & LACE
LEWIS & CLARK
LION(S), TIGER(S) &
   BEAR(S)
LOST & FOUND
LOX & BAGELS
LUNATIC & ASYLUM
MACARONI & CHEESE
MANNY, MOE & JACK
MEATBALL &
   SPAGHETTI
MUSTARD & PEPPER
MUTT & JEFF
NIP & TUCK
NOOK & CRANNY
OOH(S) & AAH(S)
PEACH(ES) & CREAM
PING & PONG
PRIDE & JOY
PRIM & PROPER
PROTON & NEUTRON
PUNCH & JUDY
PUSS & BOOTS
PUT(S) & CALL(S)
RAGS & RICHES
ROCK & ROLL
ROCKY & BULLWINKLE
ROMEO & JULIET
SAKE & SUSHI
SALSA & CHIPS
SALT & PEPPER

SAMSON & DELILAH
SCOOBY DOO &
     SCRAPPY TOO
SHOW & TELL
SLAP & TICKLE
SNOOPY &
     WOODSTOCK
SOUND & FURY
SPYRO & GYRA
STARS & STRIPES
STRATUS & CIRRUS
SUGAR & SPICE
SUNNYSIDEUP &
     OVEREASY

SWEET & LOW
TAN & SEXY
TAR & NICOTINE
TAR(RED) &
     FEATHER(ED)
TARZAN & JANE
TOM & DICK
TOM & JERRY
TONGUE & CHEEK
TRICK & TREAT
TRUTH & DARE
TWIST & SHOUT
WOLFGANG & PUCK